Mountain Range

A Dictionary of Expressions from Appalachia to the Ozarks

Robert Hendrickson

Volume IV:
Facts On File Dictionary of American Regional Expressions

Facts On File, Inc.

For my daughter-in-law
Laura

Mountain Range: A Dictionary of Expressions from Appalachia to the Ozarks

Copyright © 1997 by Robert Hendrickson

Facts On File, Inc.

11 Penn Plaza

New York NY 10001

Library of Congress Cataloging-in-Publication Data

Hendrickson, Robert, 1933–
Mountain range : a dictionary of expressions from Appalachia to
the Ozarks / Robert Hendrickson.
p. cm. — (Facts on File dictionary of American regional
expressions : v. 4)
ISBN 0-8160-2113-9 (acid-free paper). — ISBN 0-8160-3547-4 (pbk. /:/
acid-free paper)
1. English language—Dialects—Appalachian Region—Glossaries,
vocabularies, etc. 2. English language—Dialects—Ozark Mountains
Region—Glossaries, vocabularies, etc. 3. English language—Spoken
English—Ozark Mountains Region—Dictionaries. 4. English language—
Spoken English—Appalachian Region—Dictionaries. 5. Popular
culture—Ozark Mountains Region—Dictionaries. 6. Mountain life—
Ozark Mountains Region—Dictionaries. 7. Americanisms—Ozark
Mountains Region—Dictionaries. 8. Popular culture—Appalachian
Region—Dictionaries. 9. Mountain life—Appalachian Region—
Dictionaries. 10. Americanisms—Appalachian Region—Dictionaries.
11. Figures of speech. I. Title. II. Series: Hendrickson, Robert,
1933–   Facts on File dictionary of American regional expressions ;
v. 4.
PE2970. 6H46   1997   96-48660
427′.974—dc21

Cover design and illustration by Cathy Rincon

Printed in the United States of America

MP FOF 10 9 8 7 6 5 4 3 2 1

This book is printed on acid-free paper.

Introduction_____

Mountain dialect, though often humorous, is far more than the caricature it has been made over the years by lazy, lanky, tobacco-chawin' characters ranging from Lum and Abner and Ma and Pa Kettle to Li'l Abner and the Beverly Hillbillies, who live in places like Dogpatch, Hog Heaven, Hardscrabble, Possum Hollow, Puckey-Huddle, Barely-Do and Hang Dog Creek. Mountain talk, more than any other dialect in America or even Britain, is the closest surviving relative today to the Elizabethan language of Shakespeare. Though pronunciation and vocabulary in mountain areas vary, the Elizabethan English of the highlanders is virtually the same from place to place, and many of their quaint and picturesque words and phrases go back beyond Shakespeare's day to the time of Chaucer and even to the Anglo-Saxon period in England.

Though their numbers are far less today than even half a century ago, mountain people, with their rich dialect, are hardly extinct, as some commentators have suggested, and native speakers provide abundant examples that allow mountain talk to survive.

Mountain dwellers have been called "the purest Anglo-Saxons in the United States" because of their speech, though their ancestry is predominantly Celtic mixed with strong strains of English and German. Neither the mountain folk nor their ancestors speak or spoke true Elizabethan English, of course, since Queen Elizabeth had been dead nearly two centuries when the first mountain people moved in. But as linguist Mario Pei noted, "The speech of the Ozarks comes closer in many respects to Elizabethan English than does the present speech of London" and "is closer to that seventeenth-century speech than any present-day English dialect."

The compound descriptive words characteristic of Anglo-Saxon or Old English are particularly evident in mountain speech. These self-explanatory "kennings," frequently encountered in the Old English narrative poem *Beowulf* — as in "un-living" for the dead, and "bone-box" for the body — are part of everyday hillfolk speech, either carried over from the past or invented in relatively recent times. A baby in the hills can be either a *man-child* or *girl-child*, children's toys are *play-pretties*, an illegitimate child is not a bastard but, much more kindly, a *woods-colt* or *volunteer*. God is the *Good-Man* and Satan the *Bad-Man* or *Booger-Man*. The *spear-side* of the family is the *menfolks* while the *spindle-side* is the *womenfolks*, the immediate family is the *home-folks* and all relatives are *kinfolks*. *Horse sense, mother wit, thoroughgoing*, the *mully-grubs* (the blues) and the *all-overs* (a nervous feeling) are just a few of the many colorful compounds still in use today.

Many *hillbilly* (an Americanism dating back to early 1904) words and phrases thought to be the ignorant speech of Dogpatch are direct survivals of earlier English speech. *Tetchy*, for example, is not an ignorant hick pronunciation of *touchy*, as many people believe, for the word (meaning irritable, testy or peevish) is not at all related to *touch*, but derives from the Middle English *tecche* (a bad habit), which in turn comes from the Old French *teche* (a blemish). When hillfolks say *et* for *ate*, they are following a precedent that goes back to the 1300s, when English mystical author Richard Rolle wrote that "men and wimmin ete and drank" and are pronouncing the word close to its accepted British pronunciation; their use of *outen* ("This basket is made *outen* bark") may go back to the Anglo-Saxon *uthan*; and their use of *hit* for *it*, though considered illiterate today, derives from the Anglo-Saxon *hit*, the neuter equivalent of *he*, which was standard English until the 12th century. Nor is *hisn* a backwoods Americanism. *Hisn* has a long and respectable lineage, dating back to the early 15th century ("Him as prigs what isn't his'n / When he's cotched he goes to prison") and was used by Samuel Richardson in *hisn* novel *Clarissa*. Analogous words are *hern*, *ourn*, *yourn* and *theirn*. Chaucer and others commonly used the *n*-stem or weak declension in words like *housen* for *houses* and *treen* for *trees*, the standard English nouns *children*, *brethren* and *oxen* still retaining this form. Even the much ridiculed *you-uns* of mountain speech can be traced to the *ye ones* of Chaucer's time, and the collective second person *you-together* is sometimes still heard in British East Anglia dialect.

"I ain't never seen no menfolks of no kind do no washin' nohow," a mountain woman might say, and her forceful use of the double negative, though considered ignorant today, would have strong links with Elizabethan England, when the double negative was simply employed as a stronger, more effective negative. Shakespeare, in fact, wrote: "Thou hast spoken no word all this while, or understood none neither."

Mountain people, like Englishmen of Shakespeare's day, have little respect for grammatical categories if a thought is best expressed by interchanging parts of speech. Thus nouns and adjectives often become colorful verbs, as in "It *pleasures* me," "She *prettied* herself up," "I'll *muscle* [lift] it up for you," and "This deer'll *meat* us for a while [provide us with meat for a while]." Hillfolk speech is laced with direct or close descendants of Anglo-Saxon, Chaucerian and Elizabethan language — from its names for common things, to the use of "educated" words such as *dilatory*, *discern* and *proferred* by uneducated folk, and old pronunciations such as *ax* for *ask*, *dar* for *dare*, *sarvice* for *service*, *consarn* for *concern* and *sarten* for *certain*. Some hillbilly sayings also can be traced back centuries. "Everyone to their liking, as the old woman said when she kissed her cow," was dialogue put into the mouth of a hillbilly girl in a 1925 play. Investigation revealed that the expression dates back to 1562, when it appeared as "Every man as he loveth, quoth the good man, when he kyst his coowe."

That the British used to pronounce *joined* as *jined*, as people do today in the southern Appalachians, is witnessed by a rhyming couplet in Alexander

Pope's *Essay on Man* (1732): "In praise so just let every man be joined, / And fill the general chorus of mankind."

As in other parts of the South, mountain speech often uses *a* before a present participle, as in *I'm a-talking* or *I'm a-comin'*. This practice, too, has its roots in the distant past, deriving from the Old English prefix *on* that preceded infinitives, as in *onhuntan* (a-huntin'). Shakespeare used *a* this way in *Hamlet* when he wrote: "Now might I do it pat, now he is a-praying."

Afeared is a hill country word that dates back to Middle English (1150–1500). *Clomb, peart, atwixt, up and done it* and *heap o' folks* have similar ancient histories, while the phrase *back this letter for me* (address it) originated in days when addresses had to be written on the back of the letter itself.

Flummoxed (for upset or wrecked) is native to Kentucky mountaineers and may go back to an English dialect word. Another mountain term whose origins have been lost is the expression *wool* (to worry: "The baby wooled that pore little kitten plumb to death"). The Ozarkian *sull* as a verb, however, probably comes from *sullen* ("The old hound's been whupped and he's crawled under the floor and sulled up till he won't come even when you whistle to hie him out").

There are many more examples of what has been called American Anglo-Saxon, American Early English and American Elizabethan English speech. Such echoes are heard today throughout the southern mountains, including the Blue Ridge Mountains of Virginia and West Virginia, the Great Smokies of Tennessee and North Carolina, the Cumberlands of Tennessee and Kentucky and the Ozarks of Arkansas and Missouri. It is also heard sporadically in the mountains of Pennsylvania, in Georgia, Alabama, southern Illinois, and on the Delmarva Peninsula and the islands of Chesapeake Bay. Hillfolk working in the cotton mills of the Piedmont took the dialect there, and one investigator found it "well fixed on the Southwestern plains and in cities like Fort Worth and Dallas."

"Our contemporary ancestors," as the hill people have been called, came principally from the British Isles, of course, and were predominantly Scotch-Irish. However, they included larger Celtic and Welsh elements than was originally thought when the first investigations of their history were made about a century ago. In fact, the "linguistic fossils" that researchers have identified in the southern mountains are now suspected to be in large part inherited not directly from Elizabethan England but from speech brought here by the settlers from along the Scottish-English border, where archaisms such as *afeared* and *argufy* survive to this day. The settlers came first to the western Pennsylvania mountains and spread south from there, so that the hillfolk dialect basically derives from the Scotch-Irish of western Pennsylvania. Immigrants from the southern Appalachians doubtless took the dialect with them to the Ozarks and other areas.

As recently as 40 years ago a writer could observe that the hill people "have changed little" in two centuries. Only over the last 75 years or so has "civilization" courted these people, yet they still haven't surrendered to it. It is true that "many characteristic mountain words" are now unfamiliar in mountain areas, as linguist Raven I. McDavid, Jr., noted, and perhaps in another generation or two, most mountain folk will be "speaking the general vulgate" spread by the mass media, the automobile and the airplane. But the isolation of mountain people and their relative poverty — which ensure that their speech will be less affected by education — should guarantee the survival of mountain talk for many years to come, if only in a modified form or in extremely isolated areas. Certainly no large influx of population into the mountain areas can be expected to change the dialect. Despite massive federal aid over the past 35 years, poverty still reigns in Appalachia; the infant mortality and unemployment rates have hardly changed in half the 397 counties across 13 states (New York, Pennsylvania, Maryland, Ohio, West Virginia, Virginia, Kentucky, Tennessee, North Carolina, South Carolina, Georgia, Alabama and Mississippi) that are officially designated as Appalachia, and the Census Bureau has noted a recent pattern of migration to other regions that dramatically marked the decades before federal aid was begun on a large scale.

Mountain talk (sometimes called South Midland) has been described by some experts as southern speech influenced by midland, and by others as midland speech influenced by southern. Whichever came first, mountain talk, typically nasal and high-pitched, but not a whine, is often slower than southern speech and is frequently stressed very heavily. As H. L. Mencken observed in *The American Language*, "The dialect preserves many older pronunciations that have fallen out of use elsewhere, and reinforces and exaggerates most of those that remain. The flat *a* appears even in *balm* and *gargle*, but in *narrow* and *barrel* a broad *a* is substituted, so that they become *nahrr'* and *bahr'l*. In other situations the broad *a* is turned into a *u* as in *fur* and *ruther*, for *far* and *rather*. Brush is *bresh*, such is *sich* and until is *ontil*. The *au* sound is usually changed: *saucy*, as in the general vulgate, becomes *sassy*, and *jaundice* is *janders*, and *aunt* is often *ain't*."

The mountain drawl generally comes before a pause in speaking, and is usually reserved for the word or phrase before that pause. But obviously all highlanders do not speak alike and they vary noticeably in different areas. Josiah H. Combs, one of the earliest scholars to examine the dialect or dialects, was aware that there was much variation in the speech of mountain people. "The Elizabethan English of these highlanders varies but little," he wrote. "In other respects their language varies greatly, most noticeably in the substitution of one vowel for another. This divergence in the use of the vowel does not confine itself necessarily to the different states. For example, the hillsman of the Cumberlands in Kentucky says *whut* and *gut*, while the pronunciation further west in the same state, but still in the hills, is *what* and *got*. . . . But in eastern Tennessee one hears *eent* (end) while the usual pronunciation is *eend*."

Generally, the mountaineer drops the *t* in the singular of such nouns as *post* and *nest*, but pronounces the *t* clearly in the plurals of these words, adding an unaccented syllable so that we have *nestes* and *postes*. Words like *salad, ballad, killed, scared* and *held* are pronounced *salat, ballat, kilt, skeert* and *helt*, a *t* replacing the final *d*. Other general peculiarities are the intrusive *y* in words such as *hear* and *ear*, which change to *hyar* and *yar*; the final *t* pronounced like a *k*, as in *vomick*, for *vomit*; a *t* added to many words, as in *oncet*, *suddint* and *clift*; and the use of *hit* for *it* at the beginning of a clause or for emphasis, though not otherwise.

Today the drawl of mountain folk with their close connection to Elizabethan times is characteristic of the pilots of modern airliners, who may affect it to convey a feeling of calmness and reassurance to passengers flying thousands of feet above the earth. In an *Esquire* article on test pilot Chuck Yeager, author Tom Wolfe wrote of "a particular folksiness, a particular down-home calmness that is so exaggerated that it begins to parody itself. . . . [T]he voice that tells you, as the airliner is caught in thunderbolts and goes bolting up and down a thousand feet at a single gulp, to check your seat belts because 'it might get a little choppy'" is a drawl that originates, Wolfe says, "in the mountains of West Virginia, in the coal country, in Lincoln Country so far up in the hollows that, as the saying went, 'they had to pipe in daylight.' In the late 1940s and early 1950s, this up-hollow voice drifted down . . . down, down from the upper reaches of the flying fraternity to all phases of American aviation. . . . It was *Pygmalion* in reverse . . . pilots from Maine and Massachussetts and the Dakotas and everywhere else began to talk in that poker-hollow West Virginia drawl, or as close to it as they could bend their native accents."

The prudishness of mountain speech has been noted by several writers, especially Vance Randolph. "The truth is that sex is very rarely mentioned save in ribaldry," writes Randolph in his article "Verbal Modesty in the Ozarks," and "is therefore excluded from all polite conversation between men and women. Moreover, this taboo is extended to include a great many words which have no real connection with sex and which are used quite freely in more enlightened sections of the United States . . . Many mountain women never use the word 'stone' (early English for testicle). . . . Perhaps a century or so of isolation is responsible for an abnormal development of this sort of thing, or it may be that mountain people simply have retained a Pecksniffian attitude once common to the whole country."

Everyday words like *stone, bed, tail, stocking, piece, maiden, bag* and even *decent* are avoided by mountain people whenever possible because they suggest "lustful ideas," according to Randolph. Completely taboo are words such as *bull, ram, stallion, boar, buck, bitch, virgin* and even *love*. This taboo extends to harmless compounds like *buckshot* or *bullfrog, cockeyed, cocksure* and even proper names like *Hitchcock* or *Cox*. Ironically, terms like *to give tittie* that would be inappropriate in other areas are freely used (though *heart* is a taboo word). Some of the euphemisms employed for the taboo words are inventive. A cock, for example, can be a *crower*; a bull is a *cow brute*, a stallion is a *stable horse*; and a woodpecker is, somewhat confusingly, a *woodchuck*. To *cut one's foot* means to step in cow dung, as does to *cut one's foot on a Chinese razor*.

"I myself," Randolph relates, "have seen grown men, when women were present, blush and stammer at the mere mention of such commonplace bits of hardware as *stopcocks* or *petcocks*, and avoid describing a gun as *cocked* by some clumsy circumlocution, such as *she's ready t' go*, or *th' hammer's back*." Since *bull* is also taboo (two Arkansas mountain women clamored for the arrest of a man who mentioned a bull-calf in their presence), as is the word *tail* (a homophone of *tale*), a rare triple euphemism has arisen in the Ozarks for a cock-and-bull tale. There a cock-and-bull tale is called a *rooster story!*

Randolph observes some of many interesting vocabulary changes in mountain talk. "A *stew* is not a dish of meat and vegetables in the Ozarks, but a drink made of ginger, hot water and corn whiskey," he writes in *The Ozarks, An American Survival of Primitive Society* (1931). "*Ashamed,* when used with reference to a child or young girl, does not mean ashamed at all, but merely timid or bashful. *Gum* means a rabbit-trap — when the hillman wants chewing gum he calls for *wax.* . . . When he says *several,* he doesn't mean three or four, but a large number. . . . *Judge* or *jedge* is used to mean a fool or clown, and there is even an adjective *jedging.* . . . *Enjoy* is used in the sense of entertain. *Lavish* is used as a noun, meaning a large quantity. . . . *Portly,* as applied to a man, means handsome. . . . *Out* is used as a verb meaning to defraud. . . . *Fine haired* means aristocratic."

Mountaineers don't mind being called *hillbillies* by other mountaineers, but they do object to flatland *furriners* using the term; they better smile when they say it. Anyway, one of the *outlandish,* or an *outlander* or *foreigner,* as strangers are called in the mountains, would have trouble making sense of much of the highlander's speech and might indeed find it difficult getting someone to translate, as highlanders are slow to *confidence* (trust) an outsider, sometimes distrusting even natives who have *gone abroad,* that is, who have left the mountains for too long. One mountaineer told an interviewer that he didn't speak "the bestest English in the country," not having been "overfattened on book reading," but that he didn't consider his lack of education all-important: "Learning and good words may improve a man's knowings but it hain't nary made a body a better Christian person."

It has been noted that the highlander's speech is rhetorical in the classic sense, in the art of beautiful speech and effective delivery. "Many of the striking figures that seem original to the outsider are traditional ones in the mountains, having been handed down orally from one generation to another," James Robert Reese notes in an essay on the language of the mountaineer. "The mountaineer alters, adapts, recombines and uses anew old expressions with a freshness and creativity similar to that of the *Beowulf* poet who called upon his traditional poetic phrasing and word-horde to tell a tale. It is perhaps this large stock of traditional figures adapted by each speaker in an original manner, that allows the mountaineer to make his everyday talk come alive."

The use of understatement to show humor is a favorite rhetorical device among mountaineers, Professor Reese observes. Once, while sitting with two highlanders, he noticed that one man "kept getting up and walking to a table upon which lay some of the largest green tomatoes ever grown. Too heavy to ripen on the vine, they had been picked and placed on a table to ripen. The man who had grown them kept picking one up, then another, but said nothing as he returned to his seat. His neighbor seemingly took no notice, but as he stood up to leave he said: 'Carl, I'm plumb sorry your garden had such bad growings this year. Those are the sorriest-looking melons I ever did see!'" On another occasion Professor Reese "was sitting with two neighbors one of whom had given the other garden space after the latter had sold his best land. There was a noticeable difference in the amount of weeds in the garden; the one who owned the land had just finished hoeing his side. Pretty soon, Sam, who had borrowed the garden space, got up, took a few steps toward the garden, looked long at it, turned and said: 'You know I hain't a-going to put out a garden here again next year. That's two year following you given me weedy ground and kept the clean for yourself.'"

Words often have different meanings down in the holler. A wedding celebration can be called a *serenade*, an *infare* or a *shivaree*. A cemetery is a *burial ground*, and a *grampus* is not a killer whale but a type of fish bait (hellgramite). *Bait*, however, means *a large amount* in the mountains (as in "We got a bait of 'em."). Steps are called *treads*, a groundhog is a *whistle pig* and a good writer is a *good scribe*. As for a *fisty* (feisty) woman, she has been defined by one mountaineer as "maybe not fast, but a little too frisky to be nice." In West Virginia, a Ph.D. is sometimes called a *teacher-doctor*, not a "real" doctor. West Virginia, incidentally, is composed of 40 western mountain counties that seceded from Virginia at the outbreak of the Civil War, these counties voting not to secede from the Union and forming their own state government. After rejecting the suggested names New Virginia, Kanawha and Alleghany, the new state settled on West Virginia, an ironic choice, as Virginia extends 95 miles farther west. West Virginia had considered seceding from Virginia several times, due to unequal taxation and representation, and the Civil War provided an excellent excuse. Its constitution was amended to abolish slavery and President Lincoln proclaimed West Virginia the 35th state in 1862, justifying his action as a war measure. Called the Panhandle State, it has an odd outline, leading to the saying that it's "a good state for the shape it's in."

A great number of verbs take irregular forms in mountain talk, especially among the uneducated. *Drug* is the past tense of *drag*, *fit* the past of *fight*, *holp* of *help*, *writ* of *wrote*, *hurd* of *hear*, *brung* of *bring*, *growed* of *grow*, *het* of *heat*, and *seed* of *see*. The verb *rot* is often replaced by the adjective *rotten* in mountain talk (as in "They 'ull rotten afore they ripens."). Two colorful verbs are *to youth* ("The moon 'ull youth today," that is, a new moon will appear) and *to big*, to make pregnant ("He's bigged Pernie"). The verb *to smart* means *to hurt* and can be used transitively as in "Hit hain't a-goin' to smart ye more 'an a minute." Some verbs used elsewhere in reference to animals are applied to people in mountain talk, as, for example, *ruttin'* for mating: "Ruttin' time is over, Buck, fer varmints—but, by God, nor fer you-all."

Blackguard is used as a verb meaning *to abuse* by the hill people, and *to hone* means *to long for* ("I hone for her"), the word deriving from the Middle French *hoigner* (meaning *to long for*). *Laid-off* in the mountains doesn't mean "fired from a job" but means "planned to," as in "I've been a-layin' off to ketch me a eel." To get *shed* or *shet of* means *to get rid of* and *go to* can mean *intend*, as in "He didn't go to kill him."

Moonshine for illegally made whiskey wasn't coined in the hills, as one would guess, the word probably originating in England and referring to a colorless brandy smuggled in from France late in the 18th century. But a lot of *moonshining* still goes on in the mountains of Kentucky and Tennessee, where the product is known variously as *splo, stump liquor, swamp dew, angel teat, white mule, white lightning, Kentucky fire, squirrel whiskey* or *pure corn licker*. By any name it can make a man *downcy* or give him the *blind billiards*. Interestingly, the first use of the verb *stash* for hiding something is a 1929 remark about moonshine in the Ozarks: "Billy, he done stashed the jug in th' brash an' now the danged ol' fool can't find hit!"

Like *moonshine*, many mountain expressions have passed into common national use. Though it is hard to tell, these possibly include *cold in the grave* (dead), *just a little piece* (a short distance), *behind the door when brains were passed out* (dumb), *can lick his weight in wildcats, can't hold a candle to* (can't compare to), *dog me if I'll do it, I'll be dogged, faster 'n greased lightning, sharper' n a tack, madder n' a wet hen* and *plum tuckered out*.

Mountaineers in North Carolina give the name *hells* to the tangles of laurel and rhododendron that cover mile after mile of steep mountainsides. The term is first recorded in 1883 but is probably considerably older. Synonyms are *laurel slicks, wooly heads, lettuce beds, yaller patches* and *blackberry hells*. Sometimes a person's name is attached to a particular hell, such as *Herman's hell*, in remembrance of somebody lost in the mazes of wild vegetation.

Local names for things in the hills aren't widely known, but are often quaint and pretty. Peonies are sometimes called *piney-roses*, dried green beans are *leather britches*, portulaca is *rose-moss*, asters are *star-flowers*, jonquils are *Easter flowers*, violets are *rooster-fights*, the iris is a *flag*, and forsythia is *golden bells*. The serviceberry is called the *sarvice*. This plant (nationally known as the Juneberry, genus *Amelanchier*) was dubbed the *serviceberry* as far back as the 18th century and the name has a touching story behind it. Since its white blossoms appeared almost as soon as the ground thawed in spring, American pioneer families that had kept a body through winter to bury in workable ground used these first flowers to cover the grave.

Oncet and *twicet*, associated with Brooklynese, are also used for *once* and *twice* in the Ozarks, while *ary* and *nary*, which are historically contractions of *ever a* and *never a*, respectively, are still often heard there, especially among older speakers ("I don't have nary a dime to my name"). *Whurr* for *whether* is also heard, as is *allus* for *always*, *swan*, a form of swear ("I swan!"), and *to study on something*, to ponder it.

Among the oddest pronoun usages among mountain speakers is *where* as a relative *which* or *who*. Though not consistently used in this fashion, *where* is sometimes heard in sentences like "That old water where comes out of a fasset (faucet)." Another strange pronoun usage is the employment of the plural pronoun *them* with several singular nouns that are considered plural, such as "them molasses," "them cheese" and "them lettuce."

Mountain speech sometimes still employs the old form *lief* (prefer), in *as* constructions like "I 'ud as lief to shoot the sorry old critter as no." Just as favored is the use of comparative and superlative suffixes, which can be attached to any part of speech. *Beautifulest* and *workin'est* are good examples, but the curiousest is "He was the most moaningestfullest hound I ever did see!"

Thousands of other mountain expressions are recorded in these pages, some old and some new, some common today and some rarely heard anymore but still of great interest to the lover of language and the student of history. Entries are alphabetized letter by letter. In addition to the numerous sources fictional and nonfictional for these words, many noted in the text, I am indebted to hundreds of general and scholarly works, including novels, movies, newspapers and journals, especially *American Speech* and *Dialect Notes*; Harold Wentworth's *American Dialect Dictionary*; Mitford M. Mathew's brilliant *A Dictionary of Americanisms on Historical Principles*; Russell Bartlett's *Dictionary of Americanisms*; the stories and novels of Jesse Stuart; the works of Vance Randolph, Charles Morrow Wilson, and the enigmatic Horace Kephart, among many others; John Farmer's *Americanisms*; the incomparable *Oxford English Dictionary*; Webster's *Third New International Dictionary*; *The Random House Dictionary of the English Language*; H. L. Mencken's *The American Language*; and the *Dictionary of American Regional English*, edited by Frederic G. Cassidy, which promises when completed to be one of the greatest dictionaries ever compiled (three of the projected six volumes have been published to date).

In closing I also want to thank the many correspondents and friends in high places (mountain places, that is) who kindly supplied me with regional words and expressions. To my wife Marilyn, for her immeasurable help and understanding, I can only say, to use an old southern mountain expression: After all these years I still think you hung the moon and the stars.

R. H.
Peconic, New York

"*I hear America singing . . . their strong melodious songs.*"
—Walt Whitman, *Leaves of Grass*

a 1) A, pronounced *uh*, is sometimes heard, especially among old-fashioned speakers, before other parts of speech, as in "He's a-come for the receipt" or "She ran a-toward him." *See also* the INTRODUCTION. 2) Often used as a contraction of *have*, as in "He'd never a come here if it weren't for me." 3) On. "They'll be comin' a Sunday."

A-B-Abs The basics, the most elementary knowledge of anything; the alphabet or ABCs. "Sweet Bird don't know a letter of the A-B-Abs." (Jesse Stuart, *Beyond Dark Hills*, 1938)

abanded Abandoned. "He's in the abanded house down the road."

abide Tolerate, stand. "He couldn't abide to eat a bite." (Maristan Chapman, *The Happy Mountain*, 1928)

able Wealthy. "He's an able man." (Bennett Wood Green, *Word-Book of Virginia Folk-Speech*, 1890)

abody A man or a woman. "It like to scare abody to death the way he slipped up on us."

abouten About. "He knew nothing abouten it."

about to find pups Said by hill people of a woman soon to give birth. "She's about to find pups."

abroad A trip or visit of about 50 miles or more. Also *broad*. "She went abroad for a day or two."

absquatulate To depart hurriedly. The word, not much used anymore, is a mock Latin coining said to mean "to go off and squat somewhere else," as in "Your horse has absquatulated!"

a-childing An archaic English word used in the Great Smokies and elsewhere meaning child-bearing. "She's a-childin' her fourth." Also *childing*.

ackempucky Any mixture of food of unknown ingredients. Possibly from an Algonquian word of similar meaning.

acknowledge the corn Much used in the 19th century as a synonym for the contemporary "copping a plea," the phrase is said to have arisen when a man was arrested and charged with stealing four horses and the corn

1

(grain) to feed them. "I acknowledge (admit to) the corn," he declared. The expression might, however, have originally referred to corn liquor, in which case it probably first meant to admit to being drunk. Rarely used anymore, it is sometimes heard as *acknowledge the coin* and OWN THE CORN.

a-come   Come. "I've a-come for the book you borrowed."

a-coming on   It's beginning, as in "It's a-coming on to rain."

acorn-cracker   An insulting, derogatory name for a mountaineer, suggesting one is so poor and uncouth he eats acorns.

acrost the waters   Overseas, abroad. "He's gone acrost the waters." *Acrost* is a pronunciation of *across*.

actual   Actually. "He didn't actual do it."

adjinning   Adjoining. "The boy that fox-hunts with me and lives on adjinnin' farms." (Jesse Stuart, "He's Not Our People," 1942)

admire   Like, love. "I'd sure admire having that car for my own."

afeared   A hill country word meaning afraid that dates back to Middle English (1150–1500). "I was afeared to go." (Jesse Stuart, *Men of the Mountains*, 1941)

afoot   Walking, as in "He was afoot while she rode."

afore   An old-fashioned word in the southern Appalachians and elsewhere for *before*, as in "Let's get it done afore he comes," or "I'll be there afore you."

afore you could scat a cat   Very quickly. "He did it afore you could scat a cat." *See* AFORE.

after   Afterward. "They ride into town and after ride out again." *See* ATTER.

afterdinner   The period right after the noon meal is eaten; *afternoon* isn't often used. "Come over and visit this afterdinner."

after-night   Dusk, nightfall. "They met secretly that after-night."

afur   Afar. "Somebody from a-fur has to come." (Stuart, *Men of the Mountains*)

aggerpervoke   An Ozarkian term meaning to irritate or aggravate; the word is a blending of *aggravate* and *provoke*. Also *agger provoke*.

agg on   To incite or urge someone; probably a corruption of *egg on*. "Don't agg him on like that."

agin   1) A pronunciation of *again*, as in "Let's do it agin." 2) A pronunciation of against. "That's all I got agin th' school." (Jesse Stuart, "Split Cherry Tree," 1939)

aginer   Someone who is usually an antagonist, who is destructive, not constructive. "He's just an aginer."

aglee Gleeful, as in "Christmas day they was all aglee."

agley Off the line, askew or awry, crooked, morally wrong, as in "He's gone agley since he got in with those boys," or "That shed is all agley."

agone Ago. "That happened about 10 years agone here in the Blue Ridge Mountains."

agy An old, possibly obsolete word meaning aged or ancient.

ah According to Harold Wentworth's *American Dialect Dictionary* (1944): "In primitive Baptist sermons (in the Southern mountains), given in a singsong fashion, *ah* is added at the end of most clauses and sentences."

aig A common pronunciation of *egg*. "Don't put all your aigs in one basket."

ailded Ailed. "What ailded her mother?"

aim Intend. "'I don't aim to cut them trees.'" (Stuart, *Men of the Mountains*)

ain't got nary name *See* NEGATIVES.

ain't got sense enough to poke acorns down a peckerwood hole Said of someone pitifully stupid. A *peckerwood* is a woodpecker, which is often called a *woodchuck* because *pecker* is a taboo word to many hillfolk.

ain't got the backbone of a fishworm Said of a weak, spineless person.

ain't never done nothin' nohow *See* NEGATIVES.

air A common pronunciation of *are* that goes back to the 16th century or before. "'I've had nine chillun, seven air livin' and two air dead. I've lived in this same holler twenty year . . .'" (Michael Frome, *Strangers in High Places*, 1966)

airified Someone who puts on airs, is conceited. "She was the most airified woman he ever kissed."

airish Cool, cold, windy or damp weather. "Hit's right airish on them ridges."

air up To fill something up with air. "Did you air up your tires?" Also *air*: "Did you air your tires?"

allas A frequent pronunciation of always. Also *allus*. "Now the Couchies was French, my daddy allas said." (Leonard N. Roberts, *Up Cutshin and Down Greasy*, 1959)

all decked up All dressed up, wearing one's best clothes. "She's all decked out in her Sunday best."

all drug out Very tired. "A woman pore and puny and all drug out from packin' [carrying] tother baby." (Lucy Furman, *The Glass Window*, 1934)

Allegheny Mountains A U.S. mountain range extending from northern Pennsylvania to southwest Virginia that forms the western part of the Appalachian Mountains. Also the *Alleghenies.*

all get-out To an extreme degree or extent. "He's mad as all get-out." The expression is frequently heard in other regions as well.

all is In any event, in any case. "All is, things are a lot better."

all of a twitter Atwitter, nervous. "She was all of a twitter when she saw him coming to the door."

all-over fidges 1) General nervousness, the shivers, apprehension. "It is likely, too, that [Ozark hillfolk] will term nervousness *the all-over fidges* [fidgets]." (Charles Morrow Wilson, *Backwoods America*, 1934). Also the *all-overs.* The expression is first recorded in the 1820 song "Oh, What a Row": "'I'm seized with an all-overness, I faint, I die." 2) Underwear. "'I saw your white all-overs the day you went washing in the creek.'" (Elizabeth Madox Roberts, *The Time of Man*, 1926)

all-overst Used in the Great Smoky Mountains for the best (or the worst) of all, depending on the situation, as in "He's the all-overst fellow I ever seen," or "That's the all-overst sight I ever seen." Also *all-overest.*

allow Can be used to mean intend, expect, suppose, guess, reckon, suspect, admit and presume. Also *low.* "'I don't allow to work my old woman.'" (E. Madox Roberts, *Time of Man*).

all the bigger The biggest. "Here's all the bigger apples we have."

all the farther The farthest. "That's all the farther he can run."

all the faster The fastest. "That's all the faster his car can go."

all the harder The hardest. "That's all the harder he can throw since he hurt his arm."

all the high The highest. "That's all the high he can jump." Also *all the higher.*

all the smaller The smallest. "That's all the smaller I can make it."

allus The way they say *always* in the Ozarks, dropping the *w.* See ALLAS.

allus ago Long ago. "Allus ago I yearned to view the sea." (Ann Cobb, *Kinfolks*, 1922)

all vines an' no taters Used to describe something or someone very showy but of no substance. "He'll never amount to nothin'. He's all vines and no taters." Probably was suggested by sweet potatoes, which produce a lot of vines and, if grown incorrectly, can yield few sweet potatoes.

almanick A common Ozark pronunciation of *almanac,* but heard in other areas as well.

ambeer A term dating back to about 1755 that first meant tobacco juice and, later, spittle containing tobacco juice. The word may derive from the amber color of tobacco juice, plus its resemblance to beer's color and foaminess. Also called ambacker, ambacker juice, amber and amber juice. "He spits bright sluices of ambeer on the grass." (Jesse Stuart, "People Choose," 1940)

ambitious Spirited, to the point of being unruly. "That horse is mighty ambitious."

and Once commonly used to mean "if," as in "And you do that we're lost."

anent Opposite or next to, as in "The lake was anent to the cabins," or "She sat anent him."

angel teat Moonshiners call particularly good mellow whiskey with a good bouquet *angel teat* or *angel's teat*. The term is first recorded in 1946 but is probably much older. A synonym is *good drinkin' whiskey.* "They smacked their lips over that angel teat."

another guess An old expression meaning "a different sort of." "She's another-guess woman, one of a kind."

anothern Another. "Yes sir, jest believe I'll have me anothern." (Cormac McCarthy, *The Orchard Keeper*, 1965)

ansund An old term meaning sound, whole, unhurt.

antic 1) Amusing, clownish. "He's an antic fellow." 2) Lively. "That's one antic horse." 3) Used in the Ozarks for wild and irresponsible.

antigodlin Sloping, slanting. Also *sogodlin*, *antisighidlin*, and *siddlin'*.

antisighidlin *See* ANTIGODLIN.

anymore Presently, nowadays. "You know, Jesse, anymore I don't worry a great lot." (Stuart, *Beyond Dark Hills*)

anyways To any extent. "Is she anyways responsible?"

Appalachia This mountainous region in the southeastern U.S. takes its name from the Appalachian Indian tribe. It is interesting to note that Washington Irving once suggested (in the *Knickerbocker Magazine*, August 1839) that the phrase *United States of Appalachia* be substituted for the *United States of America*. "De Soto left no memorial or trace, except for the name Appalachian itself (from the Appalache tribe of Muskhogeans on the Gulf Coast), misapplied by him to the fair mountains he traversed so long ago." (Roderick Peattie, *The Great Smokies and the Blue Ridge*, 1943)

Appalachian tea Names for 1) the yaupon holly (*Ilex vomitoria*), 2) The inkberry holly (*Ilex glabra*), and 3) *Viburnum cassinoides*. All are found in the Appalachians and used to make medicinal teas.

Appian Way of North Carolina A 129-mile plank road, the longest in the world, built of parallel rows of heavy timber covered with crosstie timbers.

Though used by wagons, it was also called the *farmer's railroad*.

arbuckle   This corruption of *carbuncle* means a boil or a swelling or a sore. Also called a *risin'*.

are   Sometimes used for *is*. "Now the way you begin making whiskey, you carry your old barrels to the place where they are plenty of water." (L. N. Roberts, *Cutshin and Greasy*)

are you of a mind to?   Do you care to, want to? "Are you of a mind to go fishing?"

argie   A pronunciation of *argue*. "Don't argie with me."

argufy   Used in the Ozarks and southern Appalachians for *argue*. "He's always argufying."

Arkansas   Back in 1881 the Arkansas state legislature decreed that the state's name "be pronounced in three syllables, with the final *s* silent, the *a* in each syllable with the Italian sound, and the accent on the first and last syllables." It is still so pronounced (Arkansaw) by all natives, though other Americans sometimes erroneously pronounce it to rhyme with *dances*. In fact, the state's name was originally spelled Arkansaw. Our 25th state, nicknamed The Wonder State, was admitted to the Union in 1925. *Arkansas* is the Sioux word for "and of the south wind people."

Arkansas asphalt   A joking name for "corduroy roads" made of logs

laid side by side that were once common in Arkansas.

Arkansas chicken   Salt pork. "We were so poor all we could afford was Arkansas chicken." Also seen as *Arkansas T-bone*.

Arkansas fire extinguisher   An old-fashioned joking name for a chamberpot.

Arkansas lizard   Any louse.

Arkansas stool   A block of wood sawed off the end of a log; such "stools" were used as seats around the campfire by early settlers.

Arkansas toothpick   A bowie knife or other knife with a long blade. Most historians believe the common hunting knife was originally made for Jim Bowie by Arkansas blacksmith James Black and give him credit as being the knife's inventor. After he killed one man with it in a Natchez duel, Colonel Bowie is said to have sent his knife to a Philadelphia blacksmith, who marketed copies of it under Bowie's name. Its double-edged blade was 10 to 15 inches long and curved to a point. It was carried by some congressmen and for a time gave Arkansas the nickname The Bowie State or Toothpick State.

Arkansas travels   A humorous term for the runs, diarrhea.

Arkansas wedding cake   A humorous term for corn bread.

Arkansaw 1) A common spelling in the Ozarks for Arkansas. 2) Cheating or unsportsmanlike conduct in anything from hunting to human relationships. "He arkansawed him out of his savings." 3) To go Dutch treat. "Let's arkansaw (split) the check." *See* ARKANSAS.

Arkansawyer Someone from Arkansas, an Arkansan.

armstrong Any rudimentary, primitive tool used by hand.

arse A common pronunciation of *iris* in the Ozarks. "My arse garden is in good shape this year."

arsle To back out, move backwards. "He arsled out of the deal we made."

arter *See* ATTER.

arthur A common pronunciation of *author* in West Virginia hill country. "He's the arthur of the book."

arthuritis A pronunciation of *arthritis* in the Ozarks.

artickle A pronunciation (ar-TICKLE) and spelling of *article*. "Git that artickle and bury it in here." (Jesse Stuart, *The Trees of Heaven*, 1940)

ary, nary Ary and nary, which are historically contractions of *ever a* and *never a*, respectively, are still often heard in the Ozarks, especially among older speakers. "I don't have nary a dime to my name."

aryplane A pronunciation of *airplane*. " . . . they's two fellers here jest fell out of a aryplane . . ." (McCarthy, *Orchard Keeper*)

as 1) Often substituted for *that*, as in: "I don't know as I ever confided him." 2) Used instead of *who*: "John's the one as egged him on." 3) Used in place of *than*: "She'd druther dance as eat."

ascared Frightened, scared. "I never was ascared so bad." (Joseph Sargent Hall, *Smoky Mountain Speech*, 1942)

ashamed Among hillfolk the word is used to mean modest, shy or bashful, as in "She was so ashamed she sat in a corner all night," or "The little un's ashamed." (James Watt Raine, "The Speech of the Land of the Saddle Bags," 1924)

ashcake Cornbread that is baked in hot ashes.

ashy Angry, pale with rage. "Barb's powerful ashy today."

a-spudding round Ambling along. "He was just a-spudding round by hisself."

ass-hole kinfolks Distant relatives. Also called *butt-hole cousins* and *buttonhole kinfolks*.

at Sometimes used instead of "on." "Families used to be at the outs." (Jesse Stuart, "When Hen Crows," 1941)

a-tall At all. "Pa ain't got no right to kill him a-tall." (Stuart, *Men of the Mountains*)

at all Of all, as in: "He's the greatest man at all."

at oneself In good health, at one's best. "She's not been at herself a month now."

a-torture To be lovesick. "He's a-torturin' over her."

attackted Often said for *attacked* in the Ozarks. "He attackted him with a knife."

atter A common pronunciation of *after*. "The same man, at different times, may say *atter* or *arter* or *after*." (Horace Kephart, *Our Southern Highlanders*, 1913)

atween Between. "[It's a] fair fight atween you." (Jesse Stuart, "Last Roundup," 1940)

atwixt An old-fashioned word in the southern Appalachians and Ozarks for betwixt, between. "There's a mighty difference atwixt them."

auctioneer To auction. "[They're] auctioneerin' land off at the courthouse." (Stuart, *Trees of Heaven*)

auger a round *See* AUGER-EYED.

auger-eyed An expression meaning sharp-eyed in the Ozarks and southern Appalachians. "He's one auger-eyed son of a bitch." *Auger around* means to look all around one suspiciously and slyly.

aumost A pronunciation of *almost* in the Ozarks.

autermatic A pronunciation of *automatic*. "'I was shot down with an autermatic [pistol]'." (Stuart, *Men of the Mountains*)

autymobile A pronunciation of *automobile*. "Shore is a nice autymobile." (McCarthy, *Orchard Keeper*)

awkerd *See* BACKARD.

axe A common Ozarkian pronunciation of *ask* that has a long history in England. "Let me axe you a question." *See also* INTRODUCTION.

ayards *Cards* is often pronounced *ayards* in the Appalachians. "Gotta me a deck o' ayards." (Kephart, *Southern Highlanders*)

aye God *See* I-GOD!

babytears A common name in the Kentucky mountains for the wildflower better known as the bluet.

baby-trough A name in the Ozarks for both a cradle and a playpen. "She put the child in the baby-trough."

back An old-fashioned term meaning to address an envelope, from the days when letters were folded and addressed on the back. "As soon as I back this letter, I'll mail it."

back-actually Definitely, without a doubt. "He may affirm candid and back-actually that Tola Summerlin's was the best hawg meat he ever et." (Wilson, *Backwoods America* 1934) Also heard as *black-actually*.

backard Hillfolk often pronounce *backward* with a silent *w*, just as they do *forward* (forard) and *awkward* (awkerd).

back-back To move something backward, back it up. "Old Buck Stump made them back-back the train two miles and put them off." (Stuart, *Beyond Dark Hills*)

back-door trots A euphemism for diarrhea. "They all had the back-door trots after they et them taters."

backer Tobacco, a contraction of *terbacker*. "He got himself some backer for the night."

backing The address on a letter. *See* BACK.

backhouse Outhouse. "'Where'd you go?' 'Ah. Up in the backhouse.'" (McCarthy, *Orchard Keeper*)

backing and forthing 1) To go back and forth. "He's been backin' and forthin' to the river all day." 2) Working without much purpose or energy, without accomplishing much. "They wasn't worth the money, backing and forthing all day."

backlander Someone who lives in a remote place in the mountains. ". . . Shabby backlanders trafficking in the wares of the earth. . . ." (McCarthy, *Orchard Keeper*)

back out To dare, challenge. "He backed him out to do it."

9

back-set A setback for someone recovering from an illness. "He got up too soon and he took a back-set."

backslide To be converted to a religion when things are going bad and rarely or never practice it again once times have improved. "Recently I heard one mountaineer ask another how his sick uncle was faring. The reply was astoundingly candid, 'He's a lot better than he was. In fact he's about well enough to backslide!'" (Harry M. Caudill, *Night Comes to the Cumberlands*, 1962)

backstick The large backlog used in making a fireplace fire.

bacon up To make bacon out of a hog. "It's time to bacon up them hogs."

Bad Man, The A name highlanders have for the devil. *See* GOOD MAN, THE.

bad place A euphemism for hell heard in the highlands.

bad sick Very ill. "'He said he knowed the child was sick, their baby. But he didn't know it was bad sick.'" (Roy Edwin Thomas, *Come Go With Me*, 1994)

bad to Very likely or prone to. "Zeke was the meanest of the lot . . . Zeke was awful bad to drink." (Joseph Sargent Hall, *Smoky Mountain Folks*, 1960) Also *bad for*.

bag A highland word for the scrotum, which is the reason hillfolk rarely call a paper bag a *bag*, preferring *sack* or *poke* instead. *See* TABOO WORDS.

bagonet A pronunciation of bayonet heard in the highlands.

bahr'l A pronunciation of *barrel* commonly used by highlanders. "He's got a bahr'l full of apples."

bait 1) A large amount, as in "We got a bait of 'em." 2) A meal, a satisfying amount of food. "I got me a bait of rabbits in my craw."

baking powders Baking powder. "Tomato, cabbage, molasses and baking powder are always used [in the southern Appalachians] as plural names [as in] 'How many bakin' powders you got?'" (Kephart, *Southern Highlanders*)

bald 1) Any bare mountain top, without trees or vegetation. "Aboriginally the Appalachian forests were vast in extent, clothing the mountains, except for the 'balds,' from top to bottom." (Peattie, *Great Smokies*) Sometimes called a *slick*. 2) Can also describe a peak sparsely covered with vegetation. "Mountain folk call this growth a 'bald'—meaning that compared with the densely forested peaks, the knobs covered with Catauba rhododendron appear close-cropped." (Peattie, *Great Smokies*)

bald face A hillfolk word for raw corn whiskey so potent it wipes any expression off your face.

ballat *See* SALAT.

ballet A common pronunciation of *ballad*. "He sung an old ballet to us."

bammy A pronunciation of *balmy*. "It's bammy weather we been having."

banded up Bandaged. "She was all banded up after the train wreck."

banjer A pronunciation of *banjo*. "She had a banjer on her knee." (Stuart, "Last Roundup")

banter To dare, challenge. "He bantered him to a race."

banty-legged Bandy-legged, bow-legged. "He ran fast for a banty-legged man." Also *banty*.

bapsouse Baptize. "'I already been bapsoused.'" (E. Madox Roberts, *Time of Man*)

b'ar A common pronunciation of *bear*. One hoary story relates how an old-timer told a visitor of a certain swamp infested with *b'ars*. "You mean *bears*, don't you?" asked the visitor. "No," replied the old-timer. "A bear is something without any h'ar on it."

bare *See* B'AR.

barefoot bread A humorous name for an inexpensive cornbread made at home without any shortening or eggs. Common in the Ozarks and southern Appalachians. "I like my barefoot bread and my barefooted coffee." *See* BAREFOOTED.

barefooted Black coffee without milk or sugar. "I drink my coffee barefooted." *See also* WITH SOCKS ON.

bare naked Naked. "Them girls on the stage was bare naked."

bar-hog A gelded pig. "'And him like a bar-hog.'" (Stuart, *Men of the Mountains*)

bark To kill a squirrel with a rifle shot that hits the limb it is sitting on, the concussion killing the animal without wounding it.

barns A pronunciation of *barrens*, meaning land that produces little or no crops. "Them barns never will amount to much."

barrel-dogger A maker of illegal liquor or moonshine, who stores his brew in barrels.

barren days *See* SIGNS.

baseborn Used in the southern Appalachians for an illegitimate child.

bass-ackwards Ass-backwards, all wrong; possibly a euphemism and heard in other regions as well. "You've got that bass-ackwards."

Battle in the Clouds The famous Civil War battle of Lookout Mountain in Tennessee.

battling block A flat-topped bench or board on which clothes are beaten and washed. "Alongside . . . is the 'battlin' block' on which the family wash is hammered with a beetle ('battlin' stick') if the woman has no washboard." (Kephart, *Southern Highlanders*)

battling stick *See* BATTLING BLOCK.

bawlin' hound A dog that bays on the trail of game during a hunt.

bay window A humorous term in the Tennessee mountains for a bald head. "He's had a bay window since he was 30."

bazooka The weapon, invented during World War II, was named for its resemblance to the trombone-like musical instrument called the bazooka that was invented in the 1930s by Arkansas comedian Bob Burns from two gas pipes and a whiskey funnel.

beal To fester, be infected. "With the birth of her last baby, Clate's wife got down with a bealed breast." (Jean Thomas, *Blue Ridge Mountain*, 1942)

bean stringing An Appalachian party or bee featuring the stringing of beans in their pods. The completed strings were then hung for drying.

bear *See* B'AR.

beardy Bearded. "The dirty beardy man over there." (Jesse Stuart, "Rich Men," 1939)

bearm Excitement, emotion, agitation. "'Such bearm I never see!'" (Chapman, *Happy Mountain*)

Bear State A name for Arkansas, after the black bears said to be common there in pioneer days.

beary country Country where bears are abundant. *See* CHUNK OF A BOY.

beast 1) See quote. "*Critter* and *beast* are usually restricted to horse and mule [in the Appalachians]." (Kephart, *Southern Highlanders*) 2) Any farm animal.

beastback Horseback. "He rode beastback to town."

beasties Often the plural for *beast* in the Ozarks and Appalachians. Similar plurals, which date back to the time of Chaucer, also include *ghostes* (ghosts), *postes* (posts) and *nestes* (nests).

beat Beaten. 1) "'I heard he was beat to death.'" (Jesse Stuart, "Uncle Joe's Boys," 1938) 2) To pound, break up.

beatenest 1) Best. ". . . God rested when he made these here hills, he jest naturally had t' quit, for he'd done his beatenest." (Harold Bell Wright, *The Shepherd of the Hills*, 1907) 2) Remarkable, most unusual, most outrageous. "That's the beatenest tale I ever heard."

beat out 1) Exhausted. "He's plumb beat out." 2) Astonished, dumbfounded. "He was plumb beat out to see her there."

beat the devil and carry a rail An old-fashioned expression meaning to beat someone decisively, the saying deriving from the rural custom of having the favorite runner in a race carry a rail as a handicap.

beat the stir Beat the band. "Them fellers jest looked at him t' beat th' stir." (Wright, *Shepherd of the Hills*)

beautifulest *See* MOANINGEST-FULLEST.

bed *See* TABOO WORDS.

bedcord strong An Ozarkian term meaning very strong, like the cords or ropes used for springs in handmade beds once common in the region.

bed it Lie in bed. "Have to get back to work, can't bed it another day."

bedpost on a dress tail To hold a child's shirttail or other garment down by placing over it a heavy bedpost that the child can't lift. Mothers often did this in the Ozarks to prevent young ones from wandering off into trouble while they were busy in the kitchen or garden or elsewhere. Also called *to bedpost*.

bed with Have sex with. "Damned if I'd bed with her, considerin' her history."

beebee An old term used in the central Pennsylvania mountains for the youngest member of a family.

beef Hit hard. "There goes that boy Briswell's boy hit. They say he sure beefed him." (Stuart, *Beyond Dark Hills*)

bee-gum A beehive made in a hollow gum tree.

beeler 1) A wooden maul used in the Ozarks for splitting rails. 2) A wooden wedge for rail splitting.

beer A synonym in the southern Appalachians for the fermented mash that produces moonshine liquor.

begouge To stab, pierce, gouge. "He stepped on a nail and begouged his foot."

behind the door when brains were passed out Heard in the Ozarks and elsewhere for someone very stupid. "He was behind the door when brains were passed out."

bell cow The cow that leads a herd of cows, because it usually has a bell around its neck.

belling A big party or gathering. "Are you invited to the belling?"

belly like a rain barrel Used to describe a paunchy person, as in "He's got a belly like a rain barrel."

belly rub To dance intimately, bodies close together. "People can't dance like that nowadays. They just get up and belly-rub a little." (Stuart, *Beyond Dark Hills*)

belongers Local people, part of any group. "They ain't belongers here—jest blowed in one day about corn-planting time in April." (Furman, *Glass Window*)

benastied Fouled, covered with vomit, feces, dirt, etc., as in "It got so he benastied himself drinking every night," or "Don't benasty the child's mind with such stories."

bench-kneed dog A dog with short stubby legs, crooked and set far apart. *Bench-kneed* is sometimes said of people, too.

bendified An old word for *bended*. "He got down on his bendified knees."

benighted To be caught in the dark while traveling somewhere. "We figured on making town before we were benighted."

be proud Be glad. "Be proud you wasn't like old man Parton up here got burned down in his bed that time." (Cormac McCarthy, *Child of God*, 1973)

bereft Crazy, unbalanced mentally, very troubled. "He was plumb bereft for a time there."

berm The shoulder of a road; used in other regions as well.

bespoke 1) To be engaged to be married. "She's bespoke for." 2) To have a date for a dance or other social event.

bestest Best. "He speaks the bestest English."

between hay and grass Between one's time of youth and one's maturity; said of someone not quite a man or a woman.

betweenst Commonly used by hillfolk for *between*. "He came betweenst us."

betwixt Between. "'Did you see him betwixt us and the light?'" (J Stuart, "Uncle Joe's Boys,")

biddable Docile, pliable, obedient. "Thar's a biddable mule if I ever seen one."

biddy-peck To henpeck, nag; a hen is sometimes called a *biddy*. "He's been biddy-pecked all their lives together."

big To impregnate, get with child. "Picture of a lily trampled on the earth. That means he bigged her." (Thomas Wolfe, *Look Homeward, Angel*, 1929)

big-eyed time See quote. "They set down and eat and got through and was having a big-eyed time . . . All was a-drinking and everything was a-going good." (L. N. Roberts, *Cutshin and Greasy*)

biggity Conceited, swollen-headed. "He's been actin' mighty biggity lately."

Big-headed Conceited, vain. "He's one big-headed man."

big road A main highway. "I walk down the hollow to the big road." (Stuart, *Men of the Mountains*)

big word book A colorful term for a dictionary still heard among older speakers.

bile Boil; a pronunciation used by Shakespeare and common among hillfolk today. "She biled the water for his bath."

bilin' Boiling. *See* WILD PORK.

bingbuffer An imaginary woods creature said to be able to kill people by throwing stones at them.

bird wire A device made of wire and weights used in the Ozarks to catch birds.

birdwork To hop, jump, or leap. "He birdworked down the path."

biscuit-bread A redundancy for biscuit. "Ma baked us some biscuit-bread for supper."

biscuit weather Snowy weather, in reference to the white flour used in making biscuits.

bishop A historical term for a woman's bustle that is rarely if ever heard anymore.

bitch *See* TABOO WORDS.

bitin' and gougin' A vicious kind of fighting practiced by mountaineers in which ears, noses and cheeks were bitten off and eyes were gouged out of their sockets.

A story is told of a mountaineer . . . attacked by a large and angry female bear . . . The monster hugged him in her immense forepaws and undertook to bite away his face. But the mountaineer was determined to die hard. He seized the end of the bear's nose between his sturdy teeth and plunged his thumbs deep into bruin's eyes. With a roar the bear flung him aside and fled, leaving the tip of her nose in his mouth. The victor proudly displayed her nose, explaining that "bars can't stand bitin' and gougin'." Whether true or not, the tale illustrates the vital savagery which the early mountaineer perpetrated so long. (Caudill, *Night Comes to the Cumberlands*)

biting dog A dog prone to biting people. "'Don't be afraid, boys,' says Big Aaron. 'He ain't no bitin' dog. He's one of them barkin' dogs that never bites.'" (Stuart, *Men of the Mountains*)

black as Coaly's tail *Coaly* is a name once common in the Ozarks for the devil and *black as Coaly's tail* means very black or dark.

blackberry hell *See* HELL.

blackberry storm A storm that comes in blackberry blossom time, usually in late May or early June.

black Christmas A Christmas or Christmas season without any snow. "It was a black Christmas last year. It takes a white Christmas for a good crop year." (Stuart, *Beyond Dark Hills*) (Snow adds nitrogen to the soil and is widely called "poor man's manure" because it fertilizes the soil, producing better crops.)

black-dark night A very dark night. *See* SHADOW-SHY.

blackguard To curse, talk obscenely. "They turn and one blackguards as loudly as he can." (Stuart, *Beyond Dark Hills*)

blackguard talk Used in the Ozarks for obscene or smutty language; off-color stories.

blacksheep To steal someone's job. "I was away for a while and he blacksheeped me."

blacksnake The snake's name is often used as a curse on an enemy. "Why, you young blacksnake, I'll kill every God damn cur that steps on this grass." (MacKinley Kantor, *The Voice of Bugle Ann*, 1935)

blamedest Damndest. "I seed the blamedest sight last night." (Wright, *Shepherd of the Hills*)

Blanket Mountain A mountain in the Great Smokies. "Blanket Mountain supposedly was named after [surveyor] Return J. Meigs who had hung a bright-hued blanket at the 4,609-foot mountain above Elkmont in order to have a plain target for his compass." (Frome, *High Places*)

blanny A pronunciation of blarney (flattery) heard in the Ozarks. "He gave her a lot of blanny."

blate Bleat. "I heard the blate of a sheep."

blatherskite Someone very talkative. "I've got better things to do than listen to that old blatherskite."

blemage An Ozarkian variation on *blemish*. "There's not a blemage on her skin."

bless out To scold or chastise. "She sure blessed him out."

blind billiards An advanced state of drunkenness. "By midnight he had the blind billiards."

blind-born eyes Eyes blind from birth. "His blind-born eyes never saw his mother."

blinked Said of sour milk or slightly sour milk. "Don't drink that milk 'cause it's blinked."

blinky Sour or slightly sour. "Blinky as milk turned in a thunderstorm." (Chapman, *Happy Mountain*)

blockade 1) Moonshine, illegally made whiskey. "There is no shame, no sense of guilt [in the Appalachians] in making or selling this 'blockade whiskey.'" (Raine, "Land of Saddle Bags") 2) To make moonshine.

blockader Bootlegger. "And from that day to this, more and more whiskey has gone underground: It has been made by moonlight in hidden places, put up in smaller containers, transported in the bootlegs and saddlepockets of 'blockaders' and sold outside the usual channels of trade." (L. N. Roberts, *Cutshin and Greasy*)

block and fall An Ozark term for block and tackle.

blood kin A blood relative. "He's no blood kin of mine."

blow clear to glory To shoot someone, blow him apart. "'If you shoot a Davis dog, I'll blow you clear to glory.'" (Kantor, *Bugle Ann*)

blowed Blew. "The wind kindly blowed lonesome." (Stuart, "Rich Men")

blow fire out The old belief that a person with magical ability, or a certain charm, could heal a burn simply by blowing on it.

blow horn A cow horn used by fox hunters to call their hounds.

blue as a possum's cod This color comparison refers to a possum's blue genitals. *See also* CODS.

blue ginseng Used in Appalachia as a name for the medicinal plant black snakeroot (*Cimicifuga racemosa*), because it resembles the herb ginseng.

blue gum A derogatory term in the Ozarks and elsewhere for a black person with a bluish cast to the gums.

blue John 1) Skim milk, because it often has a bluish tint. 2) Sour or slightly sour milk.

Blue Ridge Mountains An Appalachian Mountain range extending from northern Georgia to southern Pennsylvania. Also called the Blue Ridge.

bobwhite A name hillfolk give the common quail.

bob wire A pronunciation of barbed wire.

bodacious Said to have been popularized in the comic strip about hillbillies, "Snuffy Smith," *bodacious* can mean remarkable, prodigious, bold or audacious. It is possibly a blend of *bold* and *audacious*.

body A person. Widely used in the mountains and elsewhere.

body-naked A synonym in the Ozarks for naked.

boggle Bungle, perform a task badly or poorly. "She boggled everything."

bogue To wander about aimlessly or uncertainly. "He jist bogued around all day."

bold hives An imaginary skin disease something like hives; some hillfolk believe the disease exists and is invariably fatal.

bone-box An old English word still used by hillfolk for the body.

bone idle Lazy to the bone, born that way and destined to end that way. "Hit's idle as you—bone idle 'n' slack twisted." (Chapman, *Happy Mountain*)

booger-man Another name hillfolk have for the devil. *See* BAD MAN, THE.

boogers Lice. "She looked his head over for boogers."

book See quote. "A magazine is always called a book in this region [western North Carolina mountains]." (Kephart, *Southern Highlanders*)

book larnin' Book learning, formal education. "The mountain clergy, as a rule, are hostile to 'book larnin'." (Kephart, *Southern Highlanders*)

books "Books! Books!" used to be a call to school. *Books* still means school or schooltime, as in "Books ends at three o'clock."

boomer The name for a red squirrel or a gray squirrel in the North Carolina mountains. Also *mountain boomer.*

bore An Elizabethan word still used to mean embarrass, ridicule, make a fool of. "I got real mad when he was boring me."

bored for the simples A humorous expression meaning one should be operated on in the head for stupidity. "He ought to be bored for the simples."

bore for the hollow horn See quote. "A hole is bored in the horn of a cow (having a hollow horn) with a gimlet. This custom gave rise to the epithet applied to people who behaved foolishly (suggesting a hollow head): 'He ought to be bored for the holler horn.'" (*Dialect Notes*, volume 5, 1919)

bore with a big auger To do things in a big way. "The company spared no expense on that picnic. They was boring with a big auger."

borned to Introduced to, taught about. "'Daddy made whiskey all of his life, though I don't know whether he was borned to it by my granddaddy.'" (Frome, *High Places*)

bornin' Birth. "His bornin' killed her [his mother]." (Movie version of Harold Bell Wright's *The Shepherd of the Hills*, 1907)

born on the wrong side of the blanket Said of an illegitimate child. *See* WOOD'S COLT.

borrow Used for to lend. "She borrowed the book to him."

borry A pronunciation of *borrow* in the Ozarks.

botherment A nuisance. "It was a great botherment."

bottled in the barn   A humorous term for bootleg moonshine; a play on the words *bottled in bond* for quality whiskey.

boundary   A stand of land with trees on it, or any tract of land. "We had a boundary of 10 acres."

bounden   Bound, obliged. "It's my bounden duty to be there."

bow-and-spike   A name children give to the bow and arrow in the Ozarks.

bowel off   To have the runs, diarrhea. "She was bowellin' off so bad she must've lost five pounds."

bowels   A euphemism for feces used in the Ozarks and in other regions.

bow up   Improve. "He'll have to bow up if he wants to hold his job."

bow up to   Stand up to. "Lead snaps at Blue Tick and Blue Tick bows up to his side like a fish as if to say, 'Come on, you hound dog.'" (Stuart, *Men of the Mountains*)

box house   See quote. ". . . a house with outside walls built of vertically set planks, with strips nailed on to cover the cracks between boards." (Hall, *Smoky Mountain Folks*) The term, common in the Ozarks, also means any poorly built boxlike house.

boy-child   A male child, just as *gal-child* is used for a girl.

brag dog   One's favorite dog, the one he or she brags about. "This here's my brag dog."

braggy   A very boastful person, a braggart. "They call him Old Braggy."

brag on   Brag about, praise excessively. "'I can't hep it if I do haf to brag on my own boy.'" (Stuart, *Trees of Heaven*)

brake   A term used in the Ozarks for a thicket of trees.

branch water   Water direct from a stream, sometimes a synonym for pure water.

brand-fired-new   Absolutely new, never used. "I might get your old furniture since you's gitten brand-fired-new furniture." (Stuart, *Trees of Heaven*) Also *brand-fire-new*.

brang   Bring. "'When you get back to the house, you have . . . my wife to brang the chopping ax . . .'" (R. E. Thomas, *Come Go With Me*)

brash   A pronunciation of *brush* common among hillfolk. Also *bresh*.

brash songs   The opposite of MODESTY SONGS.

brave heart   Courage. "Shorely it does require brave heart to farm in these yere hills." (Rose Wilder Lane, *Hill-Billy*, 1925)

bread   1) Sometimes used to indicate a crop of growing corn, from which, of course, corn bread is made. "I got three acres of bread planted." 2) Biscuits. "(We had) bread drenched in 'lasses (molasses)." (Hall, *Smoky Mountain Folks*) 3) To feed. "A man's got to bread his family."

bread wagon Said of a thunderclap—"Listen to that bread wagon!"—because thunder brings rain, which makes the wheat grow better, which results in more and better bread.

break To grow old, to gray or show other signs of aging. "He sure had broken a lot since I last saw him, he's breaking fast, too."

break over Break down, give in. "He broke over and smoked a cigarette."

break wind *See* DON'T AMOUNT TO A POOT.

bresh *See* BRASH.

briar-hopper An insulting derogatory name for a mountaineer. *See* HILLBILLY.

brickle Brittle, crisp, as in "I like a hard brickle pickle, no puny soggy ones." The "brickle thread of life" is an old, common saying in the Ozarks.

briggoty Haughty. "She's a proud, briggoty woman."

britches Commonly used as a pronunciation of *breeches.*

British lady Another name for the red-winged blackbird.

broad A trip or visit of about 50 miles or more, probably a shortening of *abroad.* "He just got back from his broad." *See* ABROAD.

broguin' about *See* BOGUE; COOTERIN' AROUND.

broke up Stopped, ceased. "My mother died . . . My father then he broke up housekeeping, and we went to live with the neighbors and kinfolks." (L. N. Roberts, *Cutshin and Greasy*)

broomstick An old synonym for *wife* in the Tennessee mountains. Probably from the phrase *jump over the broomstick*, to get married.

brother *See* FELLA.

brung Often used for *brought.* "He brung them over here."

brush ape An old, contemptuous, derogatory name for a mountaineer. "I want to git out of here before a bunch of these brush apes swarm down out of the woods . . ." (Thames Williamson, *Wood's Colt*, 1933) *See* HILLBILLY.

brush arbor A brushwood-covered shelter used for religious meetings and ceremonies on warm days.

brush-arbor whiskey Still another name for moonshine or popskull, because it was often used by those who attended religious revivals. *See* BRUSH ARBOR.

brush drag   A seine made of willow branches used in the Ozarks and elsewhere.

bubbly-jock   The name for a turkey gobbler in the Pennsylvania mountains, after the sound it makes.

bubby   A woman's breast. "She shore got big bubbies for her size."

bubby bush   A name for the strawberry shrub (*Calycanthus glaucus*), perhaps so called because of the globular dark-red nipple-form blossom's resemblance to a woman's breast or BUBBY. However, according to Thomas Auburey in his *Travels Through the Interior Parts of America* (1791), the word derives "from a custom that the women had of putting this flower down their bosoms . . . till it lost all its graceful perfume." Also called the *sweet shrub* and *Carolina allspice*.

buck   *See* TABOO WORDS.

buckeye   To poison fish with a mixture of the roots of the buckeye tree (*Aesculus glabra*) found in the Ozarks and elsewhere.

buckshot   *See* TABOO WORDS.

buckskin   A term used in the past to describe a backwoodsman.

budget   A bundle, a package. "He picked up a budget for Mrs. Evan."

buffalo   A name used to describe a North Carolinian favoring the North during the Civil War; the name was also given to the poor whites of North Carolina.

build a fire under   Hillfolk may be responsible for this common national expression meaning to stir someone into action or movement. Mountain people, it is said, sometimes built fires under their mules to get the beasts moving when they were standing four legs spread and refusing to budge despite every other tactic. Mrs. Palmer Clark, formerly research librarian at the Van Noy Library in Fort Belvoir, Virginia, advised me that relatives of hers in the "chuggy huggy hills of Tennessee" were familiar with the practice. "Aunt Clellie," Mrs. Clark wrote, "said when she was a young girl, loads of cedar were transported to Murfreesboro from Hall's Hell Pike. She distinctly remembers that her brother-in-law literally and actually built fires under the mules who hauled the cedar to get them going [this about 1921 or 1922 in Tennessee]." Also *set a fire under* and *light a fire un*der.

bull   A TABOO WORD in the Ozarks, where it is called a *cow brute*.

bullfrog   *See* TABOO WORDS.

bull gang   A crew of laborers. "[My job] at the quarry . . . was helping the other three on the 'bull gang' use the hand drill." (Jesse Stuart, *Tales From the Plum Grove Hills*, 1946)

bull goose   The head man, the boss or foreman of any outfit from a labor crew to a fire department. "When he's gone I'm the bull goose up here."

bull rat   A male muskrat. ". . . he had caught an old bull rat with orange fur, the size of a housecat." (McCarthy, *Orchard Keeper*)

bull roarer   A noisemaker made of a piece of wood attached to a thong; children whirl the toy in the air, making a roaring sound.

bull tongue   See quote. "For the rough work of cultivating the hillsides a single steer hitched to the bull-tongue (plow) was better adapted." (Kephart, *Southern Highlanders*)

bumbersol   An old word used in the Ozarks for an umbrella.

bumblings   Still another name for mountain whiskey, especially adulterated whiskey. "Such decoctions are known in the mountains as . . . bumblings (they make a bumbling noise in a feller's head)." (Kephart, *Southern Highlanders*)

bumfuzzle   Confuse. "I didn't know you was that sharp after the way you bumfuzzled the Superintendant's office." (Stuart, *Beyond Dark Hills*)

bummy   The buttocks. A term dating back to Shakespeare's day. Also *bum*.

burial ground   Commonly used instead of *cemetery*. Also *burying ground*.

burn down in bed   To kill someone by burning his house down at night while he is sleeping. "He's a rogue and a outlaw hisself and you're welcome to shoot him, burn him down in his bed, any damn thing . . ." (McCarthy, *Orchard Keeper*)

burnin' green wood for kindlin'   Performing a futile task. "Trying to change his mind is like burnin' green wood for kindlin'."

burnt hurry   Great haste. "He got over there in a burnt hurry."

burry   A common pronunciation of *berry*, as in, "He loves stawburrys."

bursted   Burst. "His appendix had bursted." (Stuart, *Beyond Dark Hills*)

burying ground   *See* BURIAL GROUND.

bury the tomahawk   A humorous euphemism for sexual intercourse.

bush-buster   An insulting derogatory name for a mountaineer. *See* HILLBILLY.

bush colt   Same as WOOD'S COLT.

bush up   Hide in the bushes or brush. "He bushed up when he heard they were coming."

buss   This centuries-old word meaning to kiss is still used by some hillfolk, though it is seldom used elsewhere anymore.

bust head   A synonym for potent moonshine whiskey in the southern Appalachians. Also *popskull*.

busy as a goose with nine rectums Very busy indeed; a one-rectumed goose, of course, seems to leave a dropping behind with each step.

but-and-ben   A Scottish term used for a two-room cottage in the Appalachians.

butle   *See* BATTLING BLOCK.

butt   A prominent mountain ridge, the end of a mountain ridge. "Butt is what Westerners call a butte." (Kephart, *Southern Highlanders*)

butterballs   A name for the ducks scientifically known as *Glaucionetta albeola*, but not among women because *balls* (suggesting the slang word for testicles) is considered obscene or in poor taste.

buttercup   Often used in the Appalachians for a daffodil. Other synonyms are *jonquil*, *March flower* and *Easter flower*.

bygones   The past, days past. "I remember the bygones when we were lucky we had food on the table."

by-grabs!   A common exclamation. "Well, in Baptist Church, by-grabs, you don't have to do that." (Stuart, *Beyond Dark Hills*)

by guess and by God   To do something randomly, without much careful planning, is to do it *by guess and by God*. The planner hopes that God will see it through. "He did it by guess and by God and it worked for him."

by juckies!   An old exclamation, its origin unknown.

by times   Early. "We got up by times to do our chores."

by-word   Used in the Ozarks to mean one's favorite expression, most often a mild curse. "*Gol darn* was his by-word."

cabbages *See* BAKING POWDERS.

cackleberry An old humorous term for an egg in the Ozarks and elsewhere.

cagey *See* PRUNEY.

calf-slobbers A humorous term for the meringue on a pie, or for egg custard.

call 1) To pronounce. "I don't know how to call that name." 2) To mention someone's name: "I called his name to them." 3) Mention. "The name no longer caught at her nerves when Artie Pinkerton called it in her gossip." (E. Madox Roberts, *Time of Man*)

callahooting Moving at a reckless breakneck speed. "He went calla-hooting down the road."

called to straw To be pregnant, to be about to have a baby. "She was last called to straw three years ago." Mattresses were once commonly filled with straw.

call one's name To call oneself by one's name. "How do you call your name? (What's your name?)"

call out of one's name To call someone an abusive name. "He called me out of my name."

calluses on one's feet Said of any child born in less than nine months after its parents were married; because the child would have to walk fast to make a nine-month trip in less time. "He's another one born with calluses on his feet."

c'am A pronunciation of *calm*.

camp meeting baby An illegitimate child; so named after the sometimes wild and immoral camp meeting revivals of the past. *See* WOOD'S COLT.

candle-light An old term used in the Ozarks for dusk. *See* LAMP-LIFTING TIME.

candy breaking An old-time social gathering where candy was made and couples were created by having the

25

young people match broken sticks of candy.

candy snake   A name in the Ozarks for the lizard *Ophisaurus ventralis.* Also called the *glass snake* and *joint snake.*

cankered   Spoiled, decayed, "high." Said of fowl that has been hung too long after being killed. "That bird sure is cankered."

capper   A corn popper. "Sister Nell finished popping the capper of corn." (Stuart, "Rich Men")

captain   1) Sometimes used as a title for a take-charge woman or a domineering wife. 2) Someone who excels at something. "He's a captain to tell a tale."

care   Sometimes means *mind.* "I don't care to dance," for example, can mean, " I wouldn't mind dancing."

careen   To lean, twist, bend the body to one side. "Ever' time I careened I got a crick in my back."

car house   A synonym for a garage; not heard much anymore.

Carolina jessamine   Another name for the plant more widely known as wild woodbine.

carry   To escort. "He carried her to church on Sundays."

a carrying   The amount a person can carry at one time. "He took a carrying of wood up to the house."

carry one on a chip   To spoil, pamper; origin unknown. "She's their only child and they carried her on a chip all her life, but it did prove them right somewhat being her life was so short."

carry oneself   Go away, leave. "She done carried herself to Charleston."

cash money   A redundancy for cash, money other than checks, credit, etc. "We'll make us a heap o' cash money." (Chapman, *Happy Mountain*)

catamount   An old term for the mountain lion in the Ozarks.

cat and clay   1) A clay and straw mixture used in building and repairing chimneys. 2) A rude chimney made of sticks and clay.

catarrh   An inflamed sore, usually on the hand; a carbuncle; an abscess.

catchy weather   Unsettled, unpredictable weather that changes frequently over a short period of time. Often pronounced *ketchy weather.*

cathead   A large biscuit. "It was a novel experience to eat 'cat heads' or corn pone three times a day." (Hall, *Smoky Mountain Folks*)

cat-shaking   A party game played after a new quilt has been completed. Neighbors, including young men and women of marriageable age, are invited and asked to hold the edges of the quilt. Then a cat is dropped in the center of the quilt, which is shaken vigorously. The cat, of course, tries to get off and the person closest to the point where he does escape is said to be the next person in the room to be married.

cat squirrel   The gray squirrel, *Sciurus carolinensis.*

cat switch   A thin switch, two to three feet long, once commonly used for switching unruly children on the backside.

catty-strangling   A synonym in the Ozarks for catercornered.

caucus   To talk or chatter about small things. "They caucused over coffee all morning."

cave   Any dug or natural cellar. "They went down in the cave."

cease   To decrease, let up. "That wind should cease before noon."

chamber lye   1) An Ozarkian euphemism for urine. 2) A mixture of wine and cooking oil once commonly used as a digestive medicine for infants in the Ozarks.

cha-muck-a-muck   A highly seasoned relish very similar to chow-chow; said to be a Cherokee Indian word.

chance   An accident. "It'll jist be a chance if you ever see him again."

chap   Used in the Ozarks for a male child and even a little girl occasionally, but never for an adult. "This here chap is a-cryin'." (E. Madox Roberts, *Time of Man*)

charm string   A necklace of buttons once commonly made by young girls in the Ozarks. Friends would donate the buttons and the recipient would string them together. Any friend who donated a button was thought to be a friend forever.

chaw   Generally the pronunciation of *chew* in the Ozarks.

checklines   Reins on a horse or other animal.

cheer   A pronunciation of *chair.*

Cherokee   The origin of the name of the Indian people who have lived in the southern mountains for centuries is a mystery, their name perhaps stolen from them like their land. "The word Cherokee itself has no meaning in the Indian language. It may have had its origin in the time of the de Soto expedition (1540) with the word Achelaque, modified in stages to spell Cherokee, until not even their name remained to them." (Frome, *High Places*) *See* TRAIL OF TEARS.

chewing   Chewing tobacco. "I'm plumb out of chewing."

chewing wax   An old synonym for chewing gum, especially pine resin or pitch.

chew one's tobacco twice   To think something over before acting. "I'll have to chew my tobacco twice on that."

chicken crow Dawn, first thing in the morning. "He got home long after chicken crow."

chicken granny Any woman who raises chickens for sale. "That old chicken granny cheated him."

chickens today, feathers tomorrow A saying among hillfolk roughly equivalent to "here today, gone tomorrow," or life is short. "He shook Piercy's hand and said, 'Chickens today, brother, feathers tomorrow,' and Piercy Cabe nodded . . . Cabe was dead in less than a month's time." (Harry Middleton, *On the Spine of Time*, 1991)

child-fetchin' A term used in the southern Appalachians for helping to deliver a baby. "She was mighty good at child-fetchin'."

childing *See* A-CHILDING.

chillern Children. "He married again . . . when he was seventy-seven, and he has two chillern by his last wife; the youngest one, a boy, born when he was eighty." (L. N. Roberts, *Cutshin and Greasy*)

chimbly A chimney, as pronounced in the Ozarks.

chimney shelf The mantel of a chimney. Also *fireboard.*

chippyhouse A brothel. "Your place is getting the reputation of a regular chippyhouse all over town." (Wolfe, *Look Homeward, Angel*)

chock-cherry tree A chokecherry tree (*Prunus virginiana*).

choke rag An old-fashioned joking word for a necktie; not much heard anymore.

chore A pronunciation of *your*. "Is that chore hat?"

Christ bird In ancient legend the robin's breast was stained red by Christ's blood when the bird tried to comfort Him on the cross. For this reason southern mountain people call the robin the *Christ bird.*

chuffy Fat or plump. "She's a chuffy lookin' gal."

chug An old term for a shallow depression in the road, a pothole. Said to derive from a combination of a wagon driver crying out *Ug!* when he hit one and the sound of the wooden wheel twisting in the hole. Also *chug-hole.* "That wagon came up out of that chug hole." (Stuart, *Men of the Mountains*)

chuggy, huggy hills Words used to describe the close-together hills of Tennessee. *See* BUILD A FIRE UNDER.

chunk of a boy A little boy. "'This is beary country, I tell you, terribly rough . . . I have hunted this place since I was a chunk of a boy big enough to tote a rifle-run . . .'" (Frome, *High Places*)

chunk of fire A red-hot coal or piece of wood once commonly carried from place to place to start a new fire.

chur A common pronunciation of *chair*.

church 1) To put on trial before the church membership. "He was churched for breakin' the Sabbath." 2) To deprive someone of church membership. "They done churched her for what she said."

church house A church. "There's a meetin' over at the church house."

ciphers Numbers, figures. "The [bankers] have everything down in ciphers . . ." (Stuart, *Trees of Heaven*)

citified A person who has left the mountains to live in the cities and who adopts city ways; usually said contemptuously.

citireen Possibly a variation on *citizen*, this Ozark term describes any old-time resident of an area.

City of Rocks A nickname for Nashville, Tennessee.

civvy cat The civet or spotted skunk (*Spilogale putorius*).

clacker A metal token used instead of CASH MONEY in the Southern Appalachians; such tokens were here once commonly used in company stores. *See* FLICKER.

clap one's fists To gesture emphatically, as in striking one's fist against one's palm. "He not only preached against them [the Ku Klux Klan] in his four-hour sermons, but he went out on the road and clapped his fists and preached against them." (Stuart, *Beyond Dark Hills*)

clark A common Ozark pronunciation of *clerk*.

clattermints Belongings, possessions. "The whole room is filled up with clattermints from his mother."

clean as a hound's tooth Very clean, immaculate. The allusion is to the bright white appearance of a hound's teeth.

clean ground Ground that has been weeded and is ready to plant.

clean one's plow To beat someone severely in a fight. Said to derive from the way farmers clean their plows by dragging them through gravel. "He better watch it or I'll clean his plow!"

clearin'; clarin' A social gathering during which people come with their own tools to help clear the host's land, cutting trees and brush, etc., the host providing food, drink and music for the party afterwards. "Are you comin' to the clarin'?"

clever 1) The word usually means generous, kind and friendly among hillfolk, not intelligent or sly, which it means in most other areas. "He has a good heart, a very clever man." 2) Beneficial, advantageous. "Their rich uncle promised to do something clever for them." 3) Hospitable. "She was just as good to people and treated 'em just as clever as anybody on the creek." (L.N. Roberts, *Cutshin and Greasy*)

clew To strike or smack. "She clewed him soon as he opened his mouth."

clew bird A legendary large heron or crane that is supposed to do things like stick its beak in the sand and whirl around like a top while whistling through its rectum–or so tourists are told.

cliff Cave. "The water drips down from the roof of the cliff." (Stuart, *Men of the Mountains*)

clift *See* ONCET.

clim Climbed. "These hills these old legs has clim ten thousand times over." (Stuart, *Beyond Dark Hills*)

climate To adapt to a different climate, acclimate. "We couldn't climate ourselves to the north."

clinch one's frames To attack someone, physically or verbally. "Don't let 'em clinch your frames, son." (Wolfe, *Look Homeward, Angel*)

Clingman Peak The highest peak in the Great Smoky Mountains, named not for someone who clung to it but for U.S. Senator Thomas Lanier Clingman, great booster of the western North Carolina mountains.

clipe An old term from the Pennsylvania mountains for a hard blow from a staff or stick. "He gave him a good clipe."

clod buster Used in the Ozarks and elsewhere for a very heavy rain, one that breaks down plowed clods of earth.

clomb *Clomb* for climbed dates back to the 14th century and is still heard in the mountains. "He clomb the tree to the top."

close to heaven's gate Close to dying. "'I'm so close to heaven's gate I can feel the cold gate-knob in my hand. Truly.'" (Middleton, *Spine of Time*)

clumb Climbed. "He clumb up there from the valley." Also *clomb* and *clum*.

coaly *See* BLACK AS COALY'S TAIL.

coarse voice A deep bass voice; a tenor's voice is called a *fine voice*.

coast Used in the southern Appalachians to mean a region. "A lad who has never heard of the ocean says, 'I live on yan coast.'" (Raine, "Land of Saddle Bags")

cock A TABOO WORD in the Ozarks, where a male chicken is called a crower or a rooster.

cock and bull tale *See* ROOSTER TALE.

cocked The cocking of a gun is often described by a euphemism such as "Th' hammer's back" or "She's ready to go." *See* TABOO WORDS.

cockeyed *See* TABOO WORDS.

cock one's pistol To surprise or startle someone greatly. "Well, that sure cocked my pistol."

cocksure *See* TABOO WORDS.

cods Testicles. *Cod* in the singular means penis. "'Bet me,' said the woman. 'I'll kick his god-damned cods off.'" (McCarthy, *Child of God*)

codster An old term used in the Pennsylvania mountains for a horse.

cold as a banker's heart A widely used comparison, except in front of bankers from whom one wishes to obtain a loan.

cold in the grave Dead. "Tom's cold in the grave two years now." Heard in other regions as well.

cold nose Said in the Appalachians of a hunting dog with a very sensitive nose, one that can even pick up a scent on an old or cold track.

cold-trail To follow an old scent on a trail; said of hunting dogs. "I hold him out until Brier-patch Tom Eversole's War Horse cold-trails the fox and gets a hot track." (Jesse Stuart, *Hie to the Hunters*, 1950) *See* COLD NOSE.

collar To kill a tree without felling it by removing a strip or collar of bark all around the trunk.

Colonel Once widely used, as it was in the South, as a title of respect for a prominent man.

come bad To catch a venereal disease. "Bill come bad by runnin' around with them women."

come-by-chance child Another euphemism for an illegitimate child. *See* WOOD'S COLT.

come grass Come spring. "Things'll be better come grass."

come in a one To come close. "I've come in a one havin' a lot of fights over you . . ." (Stuart, *Beyond Dark Hills*)

come off A result, outcome or happening; often a regrettable circumstance. "That's a hell of a come-off. He was supposed to pay back the money in three weeks, not three months."

come out the little end of the horn To be relatively unsuccessful in something; the horn here represents a cornucopia, a horn of plenty. "He was in business a year and came out the little end of the horn."

come over one's head To hit someone over the head. "[He] got a dead apple-tree limb and started to come over my head with it." (Stuart, *Beyond Dark Hills*)

come sick A term used in the Ozarks meaning to menstruate. "I would have to come sick today."

common 1) Said of an unassuming, friendly down-to-earth person. "He's a good common feller." 2) Usual. "They're coming again Friday night, just as common."

common as an old shoe   Down to earth, unpretentious; a high compliment to a person.

confidence   To place confidence in, trust. "He don't confidence the government or anything they say."

connipity   Spoiled, hard to place. "He's too connipity to get along with people."

consarn   1) A euphemistic curse still heard in the southern Appalachians, among other places. "Consarn it! get out of there!" 2) A pronunciation of *concern.*

contraious   An Old English word meaning contrary; in the southern Appalachians still used today as it was in the day of Chaucer.

contrary   To oppose. "You contrary him and you're in for big trouble."

conversation fluid   Moonshine whiskey. "That conversation fluid got him goin' and he didn't shut up all night."

cooling board   *See* PUT ON THE COOLING BOARD.

cookroom   An old-fashioned term for a kitchen.

cook vessels   Cooking utensils. "A tin peddler come with his pack of shiny cook vessels in a shiny black oilcloth poke on his back." (J. Thomas, *Blue Ridge Country*)

coon root   A shortening of *puccoon root*, which is a name for the bloodroot plant (*Sanguinaria canadensis*) in the Appalachians.

cooterin' around   Hanging around, doing nothing. "'What are you doing here?' 'I'm just cooterin' around.'" Also, according to Kephart, in *Our Southern Highlanders*, similar terms include: BROGUIN' ABOUT; LOAFERIN' ABOUT; PRODJECTIN' AROUND; SANTERN' ABOUT; SHACKLIN' AROUND'; SPUDDIN' AROUND'; and TRAFFICKIN' ABOUT.

corn dodger   A small corn-bread cake.

cornfield bean   An Ozark term meaning any type of climbing bean.

corn pone   Used in the mountains, as it is in the South, as a synonym for corn bread.

cornstalk gun   A kind of slingshot Ozark children make for hunting small birds. Gravel is slung at the birds from the hollow end of the cornstalk.

correspond   One meaning of *correspond* is to copulate, to have sexual intercourse, from an obsolete English word meaning the same, and the word is sometimes avoided in conversation because of this.

co-sheepie   A call or cry made to sheep in the mountains.

costive   Sometimes means costly, expensive, as in, "That's too costive for me."

cot-betty Used in the Pennsylvania mountains to describe a man who likes to do "woman's work," the term's origin unknown.

cottontop Someone, especially a child, with white or light blond hair. *Cottonhead* is a variation.

cotton-white An albino gray fox is sometimes called a *cotton-white* in the Ozarks.

couldn't hit a bull in the ass Hillfolk say this of a man who is a very poor shot with a gun.

couldn't hit the ground with his ole hat Is dead drunk. "He drank so much he couldn't hit the ground with his ole hat."

couldn't wrest a tater off'n a baby A colorful expression describing someone very weak, usually with an illness.

county pins Counterpanes; a quilt or coverlet for a bed, a blanket. "She could explain every step of making county pins."

county site The county seat. "I'd haffter walk nineteen miles out to the railroad, pay seventy cents the round trip to the county site." (Kephart, *Southern Highlanders*)

coursed Followed, tracked. "He coursed that deer across the field."

courting man A ladies' man, a rake, a womanizer. "He fancies himself a courting man."

cousint *See* ORPHANT.

cove A valley enclosed by mountains. "He clum up from the cove."

cowbrute A word still heard in the Ozarks and Great Smokies for a cow, but can also be used as a euphemism for a bull. Also called a *cow critter*.

cowcumber A pronunciation of *cucumber* dating back to early English and still common among the hillfolk.

cracklins Pork or other meat out of which the fat has been fried. "The smell of hot cracklin' and of young roast pork." (Wolfe, *Look Homeward, Angel*)

cranky An unusual word for cheerful or high-spirited heard in the central Pennsylvania mountains. "He's a cranky man."

creek and holler folks Another synonym for people who live in the mountains.

curiousest *See* MOANINGESTFULLEST.

cuss fight A verbal fight with curse words as opposed to a physical fray.

cut To gnaw or chew; said of a rat or squirrel. "The squirrels are cuttin' on acorns."

cut a rusty 1) To show off, behave foolishly. "I cussed and I laughed . . . I tooted my fox horn. I cut some rusty." (Stuart, *Tales From the Plum Grove Hills*) 2) To explode with anger. "She really cut a rusty when he told her he wouldn't go to the dance."

cute   To praise excessively, flatter. "He cuted her all right, trying to get his way."

cut mud   Run fast. "He cut mud for the woods, all of them after him."

cut one's foot   A euphemism for to step in cow dung. A variation is to *cut one's foot on a Chinese razor.*

cutting   A stabbing or knife fight. "He was arrested on a charge of cutting."

cut your own weeds   *See* KILL YOUR OWN SNAKES.

cymbling   Another name for a gourd or a summer squash.

cymbling head   A simpleton, a dunce. *See* CYMBLING.

dab-ass A common name in the Great Smoky Mountains for the spotted sandpiper (*Aetitis macularia*), in reference to the peculiar way the shorebird walks.

dabble Quickly wash or rinse. "I'll be in as soon as I do some dabblin'." (Stuart, *Hie to the Hunters*)

dad-burned A common euphemism for *damned*. "'I'll be dad-burned!'" (Jesse Stuart, "Love of Brass," 1941)

daddied Fathered a child illegitimately. "He daddied that child; you can tell jist to look at it."

dad-durned An expressive expletive. "Dad-durned my pictures if he hoes two rows of corn to my one." (Stuart, *Men of the Mountains*)

daddy oneself Said of a child who resembles his or her father. "That baby sure daddies itself."

dadgumit! A common euphemism for *damnit*!

dag A word for a gun or large pistol once common in the central Pennsylvania mountains.

dance in the pig trough A teasing remark made to someone, usually a woman, who is the last unmarried person in a family. "Looks like you're gonna be dancin' in a pig trough, Clarissa."

dangus A synonym in the central Pennsylvania mountains for a purse or other dangling object.

dar *Dare*, an Old English pronunciation that rhymes with *bar*. "I dar ye!"

dark of the moon The last quarter of the waning moon; this is the period, according to folklore, when root crops such as potatoes should be planted. The superstition is also common in New England.

dark stranger A nickname for the devil.

dauncy 1) A word, common in the Smokies, meaning 'mincy about eating,' that is, fastidious, over-nice. 2)

Weak, frail, unwell, dizzy. "He's so dauncy can't hardly walk. 3) Stupid or confused. Also *dousie, dansy. Dauncy* is said by some to be a contraction of *damn sick.*

dautie An old Scottish word meaning a darling child, a favorite, that is used in the central Pennsylvania mountains.

dawg *See* HAWG.

day-bust A synonym for daybreak. "We were up before day-bust."

day-down The time just after the sun sets, when the sky is colored red or pink. "It's all worthwhile when you look up at day down."

daylight-dawn A poetic term for dusk or darkness. "They met at the bridge at daylight-dawn."

dead as four o'clock Quite dead, refers either to the "dead" end of the afternoon, or the quiet of four o'clock in the morning. "'Finally [the bear] came a-chargin' out. When he went past, I lay my knife to his throat, then stove it into his stomach. He went off, but couldn't go far . . . He was two hundred eighty pounds and dead as four o'clock.'" (Frome, *High Places*)

deadening The clearing of land by girdling trees, that is, cutting a full circle around them through the bark to kill them. An area where this is done and the trees remain standing dead, is called a *deadening.*

dead-level best Heard in the Appalachians for one's best effort or utmost. "He did his dead-level best, but couldn't win her."

dead-man's pinch An expression used in the Appalachians to describe a bruise or black-and-blue mark one doesn't know the cause of.

deadman still A simple coffin-shaped still used by mountain men to make moonshine.

death bells A hillfolk superstition holds that when a ringing occurs in one's ears a relative or close friend somewhere has died. This premonition is called *death bells. See* DEATH BONES.

death bones The sound of bones rattling. Thought in the Ozarks to be a foretelling of a sick person's demise. "Her bones were rattling, I heard them death bones, and she was gone befoe morning." *See* DEATH BELLS.

death tick Another name for the deathwatch beetle. The beetle makes a ticking noise that is said to predict the imminent death of someone in the house in which it is heard.

deceiver-woman A euphemism for a wife who has lovers behind her husband's back.

decent Hill country people still do not frequently use the word *decent*. H. L. Mencken explained this taboo, regarding the South, in *The American Language* (1919): "Fifty years ago the word *decent* was indecent . . . no Southern woman was supposed to have any notion of the difference between *decent* and *indecent.*" See TABOO WORDS.

Decoration Day flower A name for the peony in the Ozarks and elsewhere. The plant is so named because it blooms at about the time of Decoration (Memorial) Day.

deedie An old-fashioned name in Tennessee's Smoky Mountains for a young chicken, or fowl. The origin of *deedie* is unknown.

deef A pronunciation of *deaf.* "Grandpaw was so deef he couldn't hear the chicken cacklin'."

deer eye The Cherokee Indian name for the common flower usually called the black-eyed Susan.

deer meat A synonym for *venison* in the Ozarks and elsewhere.

deers Sometimes used as a plural instead of *deer.*

Defeat Ridge *See* MOUNT BOTE.

de-horn To castrate or alter. "I'll de-horn him, he don't stay away from my woman."

derby Not a hat, in the Ozarks, but the designation for a young foxhound.

derrick An old word heard in the central Pennsylvania mountains meaning to execute by hanging. *Derrick* derives from the name of British professional hangman Godfrey Derrick, who performed 3,000 or more executions at Tyburn Prison just outside London in the early 17th century. His name is more commonly used today in the form of the motorized crane called a *derrick.*

deserted house An empty or abandoned house, sometimes used for a "haunted house."

despise to Hate to, detest. "I despise to leave these Great Smokies."

destroy To make an unmarried girl or woman pregnant. "He did destroy her, but they soon were married."

destructous Destructive. "'Dynamite is powerful destructous.'" (J. Thomas, *Blue Ridge Country*)

devil To fool or deceive; to tease. "Ah know he'd devil ye!"

devil and Tom Walker! A common exclamation. "What the devil and Tom Walker's got into you recently!" (Jesse Stuart, *The Ploughshare*, 1958)

devil is whipping his wife Said when it rains while the sun is shining; the rain is supposed to represent the tears of the devil's wife.

devil's music box A colorful name for the fiddle used by hillfolk who do not hold with fiddle playing or dancing to the fiddle.

dew poisoning Rashes or infections on the body, especially the feet and legs, that are thought to be caused by dew on the grass.

diddle 1) Used by hillfolk and others for *copulate*. "He was diddling her." 2) A southern Appalachian term for a baby chick or a duckling, or for calling such chicks or ducklings: "Here diddle, diddle, diddle . . ." Among hillfolk, the old English word doesn't have the widespread meaning of "to cheat" that it does in other regions.

didje A pronunciation of *did you.* "Didje go to town last night?"

died off Died. "The old man died off last winter."

differ Difference. "Hit don't make no differ." (Kephart, *Southern Highlanders*)

dift To strike. "Someone must have difted him with an axe."

diked up Dressed up. "He was all diked up for the party."

dilapidate Fall apart, go to pieces. "That place dilapidated so much they condemned it."

dilatoried Wasted time. "He just dilatoried around and got nothin' done." *See* DILITARY.

dilitary A pronunciation of dilatory, tending to delay or procrastinate, defer a decision. "She's the most dilitary student I have." Also *dilliterry. See* DILATORIED.

dinner on the ground A picnic. "Saturday we had dinner on the ground over by the branch [stream]." Also heard as *dinner on the grass.*

dinners An old-fashioned expression for a woman's breasts, heard chiefly in the Ozarks. *Big dinners* is sometimes used for very large breasts.

dip Cream sweetened with sugar and used as a dip for pies and pastry.

dirt land Farming land. "He wants to buy some dirt land." (Movie version of Wright's *Shepherd of the Hills*)

disablest Least able. "He's the disablest of the bunch."

discomfit Discomforted, bothered, inconvenienced. "I hope it has not discomfit you very bad." (Kephart, *Southern Highlanders*)

disencourage Discourage. "You shouldn't disencourage him like that."

disfurnish To inconvenience or discommode. "The commoner of the backwoods [people in the Ozarks] . . . may say *disfurnish* for inconvenience." (Wilson, *Backwoods America*)

disgust Hate, detest, strongly dislike. "I disgust bad liquor." (Kephart, *Southern Highlanders*)

disremember An old term meaning to forget, be unable to remember. "I disremember which of them was first." Also *disrecollect.*

diving in shaller water Taking a big risk. "You're divin' in shaller water when you talk to me like that."

divorcement A divorce. "He got a divorcement from her."

divvy Share, percentage. "You get a divvy when you sell our farms." (Stuart, *Trees of Heaven*)

doddly Shaky, unsteady. "He was so doddly he couldn't get his clothes on."

dodge times Used in the Ozarks to mean spare time. "She's workin' on her quilt in dodge times."

dog *See* HOUND.

doggery A saloon or bar. "He spends all his days and nights at the doggery."

dog me if I'll do it! An emphatic negative reply to a request or order.

dog my hide! An old-fashioned exclamation. "Dog my hide if it ain't old Dusty Boone!" (Stuart, "People Choose")

dog's bait 1) A big dinner. 2) A large amount or too much of anything, because of the belief that dogs eat a lot or too much when given the chance. *See* BAIT.

dogwood winter In the mountains, a cold period in spring when the dogwood trees are in bloom.

dogwood-winter bird A name for the scarlet tanager in the Kentucky mountains; the bird is so called because it is often seen migrating during a DOGWOOD WINTER.

dole To deal out cards. "He doled me three aces."

do-less Worthless, a do-nothing. "He's the most do-less one in the class."

dollar Frequently used for the plural *dollars*. "I made one-hundred and seven dollar out'n my timber-cuttin' job." (Stuart, *Men of the Mountains*)

doll baby A doll. "That little girl toted a doll-baby under her arm."

done called it Mentioned it. "He done called it to her."

done dead Dead. "She's done dead a year now."

done done it Finished doing something, did it. "I done done it this morning."

doney-gal A female sweetheart in the southern Appalachians and elsewhere; this word may derive from the Spanish *doña*, woman or sweethart.

donk Liquor, alcohol. "Put some more donk in that drink."

don't amount to a poot in a windstorm He or she amounts to next to nothing; *poot* is a hillfolk word for a fart.

don't care (give) a hate Don't give a damn. "Lucius, don't you give a hate about anythin'?" *See* HATE.

don't charge your mind with that Don't worry about it.

don't crowd the mourners Don't act in a hurry, don't be premature. "Calm down and don't crowd the mourners."

don't differ Doesn't matter. "It don't differ with me at all."

don't give shucks for Don't like, don't care at all for. *See* quote under SHADOW-SHY.

don't guess Don't think. "I don't guess I could get along." (Wright, *Shepherd*)

don't know beans when the poke's open Used to describe someone so dumb or ignorant he or she couldn't identify beans in an open poke or bag.

don't know but what I will I think I will. "Don't know but what I will come."

don't make a speck a sense Makes no sense at all. "His plan don't make a speck a sense."

don't that take the rag off the bush! An expression of astonishment similar to *don't that take the cake*! The words may have originally referred only to outrageous behavior as lowdown as stealing the rags (clothing) someone in the old swim-min' hole has left spread out on a bush.

doodle 1) A synonym for the penis. Also *dood*. 2) A small pile of hay; a haycock. "Put a doodle of hay in the express bed." (Stuart, *Beyond Dark Hills*)

door potato A name in the Ozarks for the Madeira vine, because its buds resemble little potatoes and it is often grown over doorways or near the front door of a house.

dope Used for Coca-Cola in the southern mountains and all over the South, where "Gimme a dope" is standard, especially among teenagers, for "Give me a Coke." The term dates back to the late 19th century when the fabled soft drink was touted as a tonic and contained a minute amount of co-caine. Coca-Cola's inventor, druggist John S. Pemberton, brewed the drink in his backyard and knew it was done when he smelled cooked cocaine.

dote on To anticipate or look forward to something with pleasure. "I been dotin' on seein' her all winter."

double cousins A term common in the Ozarks for all the children of two sisters who are married to two brothers. "John here is my double cousin."

double negative *See* I AIN'T NEVER DONE NO DIRT OF NO KIND TO NOBODY.

double shovel plow A plow with two shovels. *See* BULL TONGUE.

doughbeater A synonym for a woman or a wife in the southern Appalachians.

do which? A southern Appalachian term used when one wants a question repeated; similar to *what did you say?* "Do you folks swim in that place?" "Do which?"

dowie Sad, doleful. "When she was so dowie her hands would fair cry as she folded them."

down and did it A common expression in the southern Appalachians. "He down and did it even though she told him not to."

downcy Drunk. "All that beer made him downcy."

downgone In poor health, presenting a poor appearance. "That's a downgone Santa Claus." (Chapman, *Happy Mountain*)

down in the back Sickly, in poor health. "Pop he's down in th' back now, an' ain't right peart." (Wright, *Shepherd*)

down in the mulligrubs To be depressed. "She's been down in the mulligrubs since her brother died."

draggy Slow, often late. "He's a little draggy but a pretty good worker."

drammer Someone who takes a dram once in a while. A moderate drinker, not a drunk. Also *dram-*

drinker. See DRAMMING, DRAM WHISKEY.

dramming Drinking liquor. "The two of them were out dramming all night." *See* DRAMMER.

dram whiskey See quote. "'Now, folks could get two kinds of whiskey. They could get what they called dram whiskey. Course it was bonded whiskey, government whiskey. And they could get the other kind [moonshine] here in Harlan County, Kentucky.'" (R. E. Thomas, *Come Go With Me*)

drank Sometimes used instead of drink. "Give me a drank of water."

drap Drop. "Draps of sweat [rolled off him]." (Jesse Stuart, "Tanyard Hollow," 1941)

drap off Once common in the southern Appalachians for *die*. Also *drop off*. "Looks like he mought drap off, him bein' weak and right narvish and sick with a head-swimmin'.'" (Kephart, *Southern Highlanders*)

draps Drops, or any kind of liquid medicine. "Doctor gave her some draps for her ailment."

draw A drawing. "He made a draw of the trees."

draw a bite To make a meal. "It's gettin' time to draw a bite for the young uns."

drean Drain, ditch, ravine. "There were mountains of fine brush left in the little dreans." (Jesse Stuart, "Whose Land Is This?", 1942)

dreg *See* FLICKER.

dressed Heard in the central Pennsylvania mountains for *castrated*. "They dressed that yellow dog."

dressified Said in the Ozarks of someone dressed like a dude or dandy.

drindling Shrinking, wasting away due to poor health. "I guess she'll keep on drindlin' till she dies."

drink easy Said of well-made smooth whiskey. "It sure does drink easy."

drint Fade. "The cloth drinted a bit."

drippings Animal droppings. "I was lookin' for sheep drippings over the pasture field to see if any of my sheep had stummick worms." (Stuart, *Trees of Heaven*)

drive one's ducks to a poor market To make a poor manager or to associate with the wrong people. Also *to drive one's goose to a poor market*. "He's drivin' his goose to a poor market, Pa said." (Stuart, *Plum Grove Hills) See also* DROVE ONE'S DUCKS TO A PORE PUDDLE.

droll-natured Strange, odd, unusual. "She was mighty droll-natured."

drop-in A term common among hillfolk for an unexpected, uninvited person. "Half the party was drop-ins we didn't even know."

droprock A stalactite or stalagmite formed by the dripping of water.

dropsy 1) A humorous term referring to a person so lazy or tired that he or she is always dropping down into a chair or onto a bed. 2) Used humorously to describe the condition of a butterfingered person who constantly drops things. "He's got the dropsy."

drove one's ducks to a pore puddle Made a poor marriage for one reason or another. *See also* DRIVE ONE'S DUCKS TO A POOR MARKET.

drug Often the past tense of *drag*. "She drug him inside."

druggy Groggy from lack of sleep. "When I stay up too late I'm druggy in the morning."

drunk as a fiddler's bitch Very drunk; the term is heard in other regions as well.

dry clothes man A revenue man or law officer; origin unknown. "He thought I was a 'dry clothes' man snooping around to see if he was selling licker." (Stuart, *Beyond Dark Hills*)

dry gins An embarrassed smile. "She's got the dry grins speakin' to that new boy."

dry wilts Used in the Ozarks to describe someone very old, weak and wrinkled. "He's got the dry-wilts—must be over a hundred by now."

duckback clothes Waterproof clothing used for hunting, fishing, etc.

duckin's Overalls or other workclothes.

ducy A word, rhyming with *lucy*, that is a synonym for the penis.

dulcimore The musical instrument generally called the *dulcimer*.

dulge To dig or dig into; probably an Ozark corruption of *delve*. The word rhymes wih *bulge*, though it is sometimes pronounced *delge*.

dull as a frow Very dull. Though this may be said of any cutting tool, from a knife to an ax, a *frow* is a tool used for making shingles.

dummern See quote. "The word *woman* has suffered some strange sea-changes [in the southern Appalachians] . . . In Michell County, North Carolina, we hear the extraordinary forms *ummern* and *dummern*." (Kephart, *Southern Highlanders*)

dung out To clean out a barn or stable, mainly to clean it of animal dung.

durgen An uncouth, unpolished, clumsy person. "Most of the people around here have some manners, but he's a real durgen." The origin of the term is unknown.

dusty dark The period of time just after the sun goes down. "He called on her at dusty dark."

each and every   Every one. "Phil's Ann give it out to each and every that Walt and Layunie'd orter wed." (Kephart, *Southern Highlanders*)

Easter flower   Another name mountain people have for the jonquil or daffodil.

eat scraps off a buzzard's beak   To be desperately hungry. "I could've et scraps off a buzzard's beak."

eats good   Is tasty. "This pie eats good, Flossie."

eat something with one toe in the fire   An old, colorful, highlander expression meaning something tastes so good one could enjoy eating it even while in extreme pain. "Mmmmmm, this is so good I could eat it with one toe in the fire."

edzact   1) To do something precisely, perfectly. "I'll edzact it for you." 2) To figure out something. "She might maybe edzact what it was uneased her." (Chapman, *Happy Mountains*)

eggshell tea   A home remedy used in the Ozarks as a tonic; made by boiling charred eggshells in water.

egg sucker   Said in the mountains of a low, mean, disgusting person. "Why you miserable egg-suckin' snake!"

eke   Material that is added to a dress pattern. "She put an eke in her dress."

electric   Electricity. "'I'd druther have 'lectric than a new cookstove . . .,' any mountain woman will tell you." (J. Thomas, *Blue Ridge Country*)

elm-bark tea   A medicinal tea made from elm bark once commonly used in the mountains.

emmet   An Ozark term for a large black ant.

empty as a dead man's eyes   Containing nothing, as in "That old barn's empty as a dead man's eyes."

end   Backside, rear end. "I ought to have my end kicked." (Stuart, *Trees of Heaven*)

endurable   1) Long-lasting. 2) Dependable. "Their dreams were . . . fashioned with short endurable things." (Stuart, *Beyond Dark Hills*)

enduring   Used for *during* in the Ozarks. "It was hard enduring those days."

Enemy, The   A nickname for Satan sometimes used by highlanders.

enjoy   To entertain. "I'll try to enjoy you."

et   When hillfolks say *et* for *ate*, they are following a precedent that goes back to the 1300s (when English author Richard Rolle wrote that "men and wimmen et and drank") and are pronouncing the word close to its accepted British pronunciation. "He may affirm . . . that Tola Summerlin's was the best hawg meat he ever et." (Wilson, *Backwoods America*)

eveglom   An old term for evening twilight.

evenin'   Used by hillfolk for the long period between noontime and sunset, not just for the short period before night.

everen   Used by hillfolk for whenever or when. "Everen we went there, I visited them." Also *everwhen*.

ever fetchin' one of them   An emphatic way that highlanders say *every one of them*. "I'll get ever fetchin' one of them!"

everhow   A way to say *however* in the Ozarks. "Everhow they do it is all right with me, providin' they jest do it quiet."

ever I seed   An Ozarkian way of saying *that I've ever seen*. "There's the travellinest hosses ever I seed." (Kephart, *Southern Highlanders*)

everly   An old southern Appalachian word for *always*. "I everly stop in there for a drink."

ever-what   Whatever. "Ever-what she had burned to the ground."

everwhen   *See* EVEREN.

everwhere   Frequently used in the southern Appalachians for *wherever*. "Everwhere we go we see them planting."

everwhich   Used mainly in the Ozarks and southern Appalachians for *whichever*. "Everwhich you choose you can have."

ever-which-a-ways   In every direction. "His hair had a habit of sticking out ever-which-a-ways." (Chapman, *Happy Mountain*)

everwho   Commonly used for *whoever* in the Ozarks. "They's a law in Arkansas pertectin' foxes, and if anyone should ever get caught it would be unfortunate for everwho owned the dawgs." (Wilson, *Backwoods America*)

every dog for his dinner   Every man for himself.

every little whipstitch Often, every instant. "He goes over there every little whipstitch."

everyone to their liking, as the old woman said when she kissed her cow An old saying of hill people that actually dates back to 16th-century England, when it appeared as, "Every man as he loveth, quoth the good man, when he kyst his coowe."

exaltify Exalt. "There's no need to exaltify him to me."

excape A common pronunciation of *escape* in the Ozarks. "He excaped from jail."

extry Extra. "We got some extry sody (soda) if you want some."

ezactly A pronunciation of *exactly*.

fair up Clear up. "This rainy weather will fair up by tomorrow."

fallen weather Rain, snow, hail, fog, etc. "Ye know the first day ye come out here how the smoke was goin' to the ground. That's a good sign of fallen weather." (Stuart, *Hie to the Hunters*)

fall grape A southern Appalachian term for a wild grape, such as the fox grape.

fallin' away Losing weight, becoming sickly. "She's been fallin' away since her husband died."

fall out To disagree; a term used in other regions as well. "He fell out with his brother."

falltime Autumn. "I saw her in the falltime."

fambly A pronunciation of *family*. "Course she was proud of her fambly, and just like any woman in the hills she wouldn't have nothing to do with men strangers." (L. N. Roberts, *Cutshin and Greasy*)

far and squar Fair and square. "Far and squar is the way we live around here."

farewell summer A colorful name in the southern Appalachians for the fall flower better known nationally as the aster. Also *goodbye summer*.

farmer's railroad *See* APPIAN WAY OF NORTH CAROLINA.

farm liquor Ordinary moonshine, unaged, without color and with great potency. Also called *field whiskey*.

farplace Fireplace. "We had a big farplace where my mother cooked . . ." (L. N. Roberts, *Cutshin and Greasy*)

fast as skim milk through a tow sack Very fast, the way thin skim milk would leak out after being poured into a coarse burlap sack.

faster 'n greased lightning Speedy, said of someone or something very fast.

fastly An old-fashioned Ozark word meaning firmly. "Hold on fastly to your faith."

fat pine A knot, splinter or branch of various pine trees that is used as kindling. Also called *lightwood*.

favorance Resemblance. "There's a strong favorance between them."

feather crown A belief among highlanders that when someone dies the feathers inside his bed pillow sometimes form a circle or crown, indicating that the dead person is in heaven.

feather into 1) To shoot someone, physically do someone harm, or do something with great vigor. The commonly used Ozarkian term dates back to early England, when it strictly meant to shoot someone with the arrow from a longbow so forcefully that the feather on the end of the arrow entered the person's body. 2) Attack. "He feathered into the whole bunch of them."

feel of Feel. "They waited for Doc Minton to feel of Willard's ticker." (Stuart, *Beyond Dark Hills*)

feist To flirt, move provocatively. "She feisted around all night at the party."

fella A pronunciation of *fellow*, a common form of address in the mountains, as in *brother*. "'And how can you not like a man, even a city fella, who talks to trout when he fishes . . .'" (Middleton, *Spine of Time*)

fellowly Understanding, companionable.

female person A redundancy for female. "He had great respect for every female person."

fence lifter A heavy rain. "It rained hard all night—a real fence lifter."

fernent A Scottish word sometimes heard in the southern Appalachians for *near* or *nearly*. "She was fernent the house last time I saw her."

ferricadouzer An old word used in the central Pennsylvania mountains for a sound beating.

fertili An Ozark word for *fertilizer*. "He used plenty of fertili on that crop." *See* FERTILIZE.

fertilize Often used as a word for commercial fertilizer. "Their fertilize is the best."

fetched up Came up to, appeared in front of. "Finally he fetched up in front of the meatcase." (McCarthy, *Child of God*)

fetching stick A long stick with a forked end that Ozark storekeepers once commonly used to reach items on high shelves.

feudin' kinfolks Not relatives but close allies in a feud or cause. "We got a hundred behind us, countin' feudin' kinfolks."

few Some, a portion, especially at the table. "I'll have a few more of them cabbage [another helping]." (Kephart, *Southern Highlanders*)

fiddle dancing   Dancing to music made by a fiddle, a popular diversion among hillfolk.

Fiddler's Green   A paradise said to be seven miles from the coolest side of Hell, where there is fiddling and dancing and wine and all kinds of fun all of the time.

field whiskey   Same as FARM LIQUOR.

figger   An Ozark pronunciation of *figure*. "I figger he'll be here today." The same pronunciation is used today in England.

fight a circle saw   To be brave and daring, afraid of nothing. "Dave would fight a circle saw if it insulted him."

fightin'est   The most aggressive, scrappiest. "Buck's the fightin'est dog around."

fight one's face   To eat ravenously. "I feel like I could fight my face, too . . . Gives a body a hankerin' for grub to walk up here." (Stuart, *Hie to the Hunters*)

filth   A synonym for unwanted weeds and brush in the southern Appalachians. Land with weeds and brush is often called *filth land*.

fine-haired   Someone too educated, fine-mannered, aristocratic, fastidious, conceited. Fine hair was once supposed to be a physical characteristic of a gentleman. "That fine-haired son-of-a-bitch better watch himself."

fine voice   *See* COARSE VOICE.

fireboard   Another word for a mantelpiece above a fireplace. *See* CHIMNEY SHELF.

fire coal   An ember in a fire. "The fire coals were glowing very brightly."

fire in the hole!   Moonshiners in the southern Appalachians shout this warning in a high-pitched voice when federal agents are sighted in the vicinity. The words were originally a miner's warning of impending danger.

first-handed   At first hand. "We want [the confession] first-handed here. You can give it second-handed to the Devil." (Stuart, *Beyond Dark Hills*)

fishhooks in one's pockets   To be very cheap. The expression may have originated in the Ozarks, but Long Island, New York sea captain Samuel Mulford lined his pockets with fishhooks to foil pickpockets when he visited London before the American Revolution. (His ploy worked.)

fishworm   A synonym for an earthworm in West Virginia.

fist   To hit or beat someone with the fists. "He went to jail for fisting his old woman till she didn't look like herself."

fisty (feisty) woman   Defined by one highlander as "maybe not fast, but a little too feisty to be nice."

fit Fought. "I fit him last night. I will fight him anytime."

fittin Fitting, suitable, proper. "It's a more fittin place to live." (Stuart, "Tanyard Hollow")

fitty Appropriate, fit. "That outfit ain't fitty to wear fer Hell."

fixin' Intending. "I'm fixin' to go there next week."

fixy 1) Fancy, full of frills. "All these here fixy contrapshuns." (J. Thomas, *Blue Ridge Country*). 2) Well-groomed, fastidious in appearance; said of a neatly kept person, often a young woman.

flag Another name for the common iris flower.

flags A term sometimes used for *bullrushes* when women are present, because *bull* is considered an offensive word with sexual connotations.

flat as a flitter Flat as a pancake, a *flitter* being the name for a pancake.

flatlander One who is not from the mountains, a *furriner*. "'Get's to you, eh, flatlander,' he said." (Middleton, *Spine of Time*)

flatwoods Level lands in the Ozarks that have been cleared of timber.

flicker A name once common in the southern Appalachians for the scrip or coins paid by coal companies to their workers. Flicker only brought 90 cents to the dollar anywhere else but at the company store. It was also called CLACKER; DREG; and STICKERS.

flippy-whippet A term Ozark hillfolk reserve for silly, flighty people. "We don't want her around here with her flippy-whippet ways."

flitter *See* FLAT AS A FLITTER.

flog Used to describe the beating of a rooster's wing. "One rooster flogged another rooster for getting too near his hens." (Stuart, *Hie to the Hunters*)

flowzy Unkempt, messy. "Her hair was all flowzy and her dress was torn."

flummoxed Upset or irked; a word used by Kentucky mountaineers that has been traced back to an old English dialect word.

flux A synonym, used primarily in the southern Appalachians, for dysentery. Sometimes called *the bloody flux*.

fly poison A lily-like plant (*Amianthium muscaetoxicum*) used to make insecticides. "The curious big fly poison lit up the sward with flecks of white." (Peattie, *Great Smokies*)

follow to the middle pits of hell Be completely loyal to. "They'd foller him to the middle pits of hell."

fool with me and there'll be a new face in hell tomorrow A threat heard in the Ozarks.

foot-whacking Running very noisily. "There he went foot-whackin' away from them federal men."

for Because of. "He had smoked his cigar so short that we couldn't see it for his mustache." (Jesse Stuart, "Bury Your Dead," 1942)

for a fact Certainly. "I know for a fact he did it."

forard *See* BACKARD.

foreigner *See* FURRINER.

for to A common redundancy. "We cut the stove wood and ricked it for to season a few days." (Stuart, *Men of the Mountains*)

forty-gallon Baptists A historical term for mountaineers who believed one must be totally immersed in water to be properly baptized. Those who believed a symbolic sprinkling of water would do were called *half-pint Baptists*.

for why Often heard in the southern Appalachians for *why*. "For why did she go with him?"

fotch Fetch. "Fotch me that flour."

fotch-on Said of a store-bought product, one that is brought from somewhere else, not in the area. "Damn this fotch-on kraut that comes in tin cans." (Kephart, *Southern Highlanders*)

four rooms and a path A name used in coal towns throughout the mountains for the substandard houses that the coal companies provided their workers. The "path" led to the privy in the back yard.

fox and dogs A children's game in which one player is chased by the others. "When we played fox and dogs, Big Andy was usually the fox. He could outrun the rest of us over the big meadows on the Uplands, through the woods and down the hollow." (Stuart, *Beyond Dark Hills*)

foxfire 1) An organic luminescence on decayed wood, usually caused by fungi. 2) Any of the fungi that cause the luminescence on decaying wood.

foxhead Another Ozarkian name for potent moonshine, its origin unknown.

fox-hound *See* HOUND.

foxpath A narrow footpath. "The little foxpath that wound up the steep bluff." (Stuart, "Whose Land Is This?")

fraction In the southern Appalachians, a *fraction* is a disturbance or fight, a fracas. "I don't know how the fraction began, but Os feathered into Dan and Phil, feeding them lead." (Kephart, *Southern Highlanders*)

fractious Bad tempered, unruly, rude in manner. "He's always been a nervous fractious man."

fraid hole A cyclone cellar, any protected cave or hole in the ground where people can take refuge from a tornado and other violent windstorms.

frame Skeleton. "They say the frames of them dead Rebels laid up there in the crevices till the meat dropped offen their frames." (L. N. Roberts, *Cutshin and Greasy*)

franzied Crazy, delirious. "All those kids made her franzied."

frazzle-headed Used to describe a man whose hair is cut unevenly or is not combed.

freckled as a turkey egg Heard among hillfolk in the Ozarks for a person with lots of freckles.

frequent Common, abundant. "Deers was purty frequent in that country." (L. N. Roberts, *Cutshin and Greasy*)

fringe bush *Chionanthus virginicus*, a small tree or shrub with fringed winged pods and clusters of white flowers. "The sourwood, the fringe bush, and the mountain laurel are understory trees." (Peattie, *Great Smokies*)

fritter-minded Erratic, flighty, frivolous. "First you know you'll be fritter-minded as an outlander." (Chapman, *Happy Mountains*)

frog sticker A long-bladed pocket knife with a sharp point.

from can see to can't see From dawn until dark. "We worked from can see to can't see."

fruitjar-sucker An insulting, derogatory name for a mountaineer, referring to the Mason jars moonshine is sold in.

fruit-orchard A redundancy for orchard.

full-handed Well-to-do. "He had aplenty—a full-handed man."

fun 1) To joke. "Aaron laughed at me. He thought I was funnin'." (Jesse Stuart, "The Hangin' of W.B.," 1938). 2) To hoax. "I thought he was just funnin' me a little." (Stuart, *Men of the Mountains*)

funeral Funeral oration. "The preacher preached a long funeral under the tree." (Stuart, *Men of the Mountains*)

fur 1) A pronunciation of *far*. "It's a darn fur piece to walk." 2) A pronunciation of *for*. "Who are you buyin' that fur?"

furnish A bill or an account for supplies in a general store; from the verb *furnish*, to supply. "The storekeeper said he'd put it on my furnish."

furriner A foreigner, an outlander, a stranger to the hills.

furse A pronunciation of *fuss*; rhymes with *purse*. "Your Pa will furse with me." (Stuart, *Trees of Heaven*)

gaggle   An Ozark pronunciation of *gargle*.

gaily   Spirited, lively. "That's a gaily horse she rides."

gaint   A highlander pronunciation of *gaunt*. "Pa has begun to look gaint."

gal-child   *See* BOY-CHILD.

gale   A name given to an old, recently gelded bull in the central Pennsylvania mountains.

gallery   Hillfolk prefer using this synonym for porch or veranda.

galloopus   A legendary eagle-like black bird of the hills which laid square eggs and whose dung created extremely fertile soil in certain areas.

gallynipper   Once used to describe only a huge mosquito, *gallynipper* is now applied to many large flying insects.

gal-person   *See* MAN-PERSON.

gander berry   A very large huckleberry variety said to be favored by ganders.

gap   Gate. "He came in through the front gap."

garbroth   Worthless or poor in quality, like broth made from the gar, which is regarded as an inferior fish.

gather-all   A gathering of people, as in the title of Jesse Stuart's short story "Gather-all in the Hollow," 1942.

gaum   1) To smear. "He gaumed molasses all over her." 2) Sticky, smeared. "The little un's all gaumed up." Also *gom, gorn.*

gee haw   To disagree. "All this here gee hawin', boltin', and kickin' 'mongst the married folks." (Wright, *Shepherd*)

geik   A word for a homemade fiddle in the central Pennsylvania mountains.

gellyon   A blend of *gel*ding and stal*lion* used in the central Pennsylvania mountains for a castrated horse.

generally always Usually. "Richmond generally always comes in after his mail Tuesday afternoon." (Wilson, *Backwoods America*)

generation A large family, a kind, a breed, a race. "There's a powerful generation of them Wilsons."

gentle To make tame. "He was skittish as a yearling colt and no hand could gentle him." (Chapman, *Happy Mountain*)

get down and stay with us A southern Appalachian invitation to a stranger to spend the night that dates back to the days of horseback when strangers rode up to a house.

get offen Get off. "Get offen my land."

get on to To accuse, chide, find fault with. "He got on to him about being late to work all the time."

get shut of Get rid of. "[They'd see him] slouched and solitary, the rifle hanging in his hand as if it were a thing he could not get shut of." (McCarthy, *Child of God*) Also *get shet* (shed) *of*.

getting less and leaster Getting smaller and smaller. "Our savings are getting less and leaster."

getting sweet See quote. "'It sweats,' Spring told him. 'The fox does. They [the dogs] can smell him better after he's been running awhile. That's 'getting sweet'." (Kantor, *Bugle Ann*)

ghostes *See* BEASTIES.

giant powder Powerful dynamite used by builders and demolition crews. Pronounced *joint powder*.

giasticutus Another legendary animal of the mountains, this one a huge bird with a 50-foot wingspread that can fly off with cattle.

gimlet-assed Used in the Ozarks to mean thin. "Look at that gimlet-assed son-of-a-bitch."

gin If. "I'll ax the woman gin she can git ye a bite." (Kephart, *Southern Highlanders*)

gin gang A gang of laborers. "Three fifty [dollars] for ten hours on the gin gang . . . The 'bull gang' it was called by many." (Stuart, *Beyond Dark Hills*)

girl-child The name for a female baby among the hillfolk.

give a lick and a promise To fix something so that it will work temporarily, until it can be fixed properly. "I gave the car a lick and a promise, crossing my fingers."

give down Break down. "I gave down on marching the light miles and carrying the heavy pack." (Stuart, *Beyond Dark Hills*)

give 'em Jesse Give him hell, give him the dickens.

given up Acknowledged as. "She's given up to be the prettiest girl in these parts."

give-out 1) An announcement. "The give-out at church told about their marriage." 2) Very tired, having no strength left. "I'm about to give out." 3) Give up, gave up. "I reckon you give out expecting me to come."

give tittie To breastfeed a child. Not a taboo expression, even though words as seemingly innocuous as STONE (which can mean testicles) are avoided by women.

glede An old word in the central Pennsylvania mountains for a red-hot coal carried from one cabin to another to start fires.

glib Said in the Ozarks of brisk active movements. "He's ninety years old but pretty glib." Does not mean quick of speech as it does elsewhere. Sometimes seen as *glib as quail.*

glomb To poke. "He would glomb me in the eyes with his fingers." (Stuart, *Men of the Mountains*)

glory Boast. "I'm a hillbilly all right, and they needn't to glory their old flat lands to me." (Kephart, *Southern Highlanders*)

go *See* GO TO.

goat meat A euphemism highlanders use for deer meat when it is hunted and killed out of legal hunting season. Also *goat mutton.*

God-awfulest The worst. "That's the God-awfulest music I ever heard."

God respects you if you work, but He loves you if you sing A charming old saying from the Great Smoky Mountains.

God's acre A piece of land in the Ozarks from which crops are given to the church. In other places it is called *God's Little Acre*, as in Erskine Caldwell's famous 1933 novel of that name.

goin' drink till the world looks little Going to get drunk until all my problems seem like nothing at all.

golden bells Another name for forsythia in the mountains.

golly-whopper Anything big or extraordinary, a huge specimen of something. "That's a golly-whopper of a bass he caught."

gone abroad Left the mountains for a long time. "Leon's gone abroad two years now."

gone back on his (her) raisin' To do something one has been taught never to do by one's parents or family.

goober-grabber 1) A very stingy person. 2) A bold wanton, one who would grab for a man's goobers (testicles). *Goober* is, of course, a synonym for peanut.

gooch To dig, gouge. "What're you laughin' at, son?" said Mary, gooching him roughly in the ribs." (Wolfe, *Look Homeward, Angel*)

good Sometimes used in the sense of complete or completely. "They stayed out playing till good dark."

gooder Mostly a mountain term for a good one or a good thing. "That's a real gooder!" ("That's a good joke!")

good honk Correspondent Madolin Johnson Wells advises that her mother, who hailed from Arkansas, used this expression when startled or upset, as in "Good honk (pronounced *good haohnk*), Lon, what've you done?" In rare cases of extreme emphasis, Mrs. Wells writes, her mother would say, "'Great honk!' which conjured images of a strange bird or a mythical god."

good liver A man who made a good living out of his land, who was prosperous.

goodlye A pronunciation of *goodly* in the Ozarks, just as *quickly* is pronounced *quick-lye*.

Good Man, The A reverent name hillfolk use for God. *See also* BAD MAN, THE.

good scribe A good writer. "I like his stories; he's a good scribe."

google A name for the throat, or for the Adam's apple.

goomer To bewitch; a *goomer-doctor* is a witch doctor.

goose drownder See TOAD STRANGLER.

go out to themselves Said in the southern Appalachians of newly-weds who go out to establish a new residence. "They've gone out to themselves, away from all the family."

goozle *See* GOOGLE.

go to Intend. "He didn't go to kill him."

go to hell and fry in your own lard The expletive is an old one once common in hill country. "The others knew from the drawl with which he spoke that he was enraged almost beyond control: 'Well, you can go to hell and fry in your own lard.'" (Kantor, *Bugle Ann*)

go to the brush Go to the bathroom out in the woods, though the term is also used now by those who have indoor plumbing.

got up Got to be, reached the age of. "'The horse we owned when I got up fourteen and fifteen was full of tricks.'" (R. E. Thomas, *Come Go With Me*)

got up any size Became more than an infant. "Alex . . . has lived here in Harlan County ever since he got any size." (L. N. Roberts, *Cutshin and Greasy*)

government liquor Legally made liquor as opposed to MOONSHINE.

gowrow A dangerous mythical monster once widely believed to live in the Ozark wilds.

governmint A common pronunciation of *government* in hill country.

grabble To dig up potatoes from a row with one's hands, leaving the plants intact.

grain A little, a bit. "You might o' been a grain warmer about hit . . ." (Wright, *Shepherd*)

grampus Not a killer whale but a type of fish bait (hellgrammite).

grandma To cut down and steal timber from someone else's property; perhaps so called because an anonymous highlander who stole timber explained that he got it from "grandma's" place. Another theory has this unusual word deriving from an old story or joke about a man accused of stealing another's timber and finally admitting that "Grandmaw might have taken a few sticks." A *grandmawer* is someone who steals timber.

Grand Old Man of the Campfire and Long Trail *See* MOUNT KEPHART.

grand-rascal An old term for a confidence man. "That grand-rascal got all their money."

grannie woman 1) A woman who delivers babies, a midwife. "Grandma was a grannie woman and a charm doctor." (Stuart, "Last Roundup") 2) A simple old man.

grape-vineyard A redundancy for *vineyard*.

grasswiddy Grass widow, an old term for a divorced woman.

grave house See quote. "Many [mountain cemeteries] have 'grave houses'—rude log and clapboard shutters—that mountaineers customarily erect over and around the graves of their relations." (*Federal Writers Program Guide to Kentucky*, 1939)

gravel To annoy or embarrass someone. "She gravels everybody with all her airs."

gravel flipper A term heard in the southern Appalachians for a slingshot. "He hunted squirrels with his gravel flipper."

grave rock A gravestone, headstone or wooden grave marker. "The grave rocks were so old they looked like stones in the field."

greasy bean A long-podded bean variety (*Phaseolus vulgaris*) that has been grown in the Ozarks since pre–Civil War times.

greasy door family Said of a family that has recently slaughtered its hogs, thus leaving hog grease from their hands on the doorknobs and doors.

great long Very long, as in "He's gone a great long time."

Great Smokies   The area takes its name from the Cherokee name for the mountains meaning "The Place of the Blue Smoke." Also called the Great Smoky Mountains.

gredge   Grudge. "Hit's jist somebody who has a gredge agin the blockader." (Kephart, *Southern Highlanders*) See BLOCKADER.

green   Tease or ridicule. "Don't you green Sis or you'll deal with me."

green out   Cheat, swindle. "No how Shine greened Tom outen a good shotgun." (E. Madox Roberts, *Time of Man*)

green up   Used in the mountains to describe trees and plants that have begun to put out new growth in the spring. "The dogwoods are all greened up."

gritchel   An old term for a valise or traveling bag.

gritted bread   Corn bread that is made mainly from corn grated on a *gritter*.

groundhog   To squirrel away or pocket money, especially in a poker game. It refers to *hogging* money away in a hole in the ground.

groundhog case   A last chance, a last resort, a do or die situation. "We got to win this one for the coach; it's a groundhog case with us."

grouty   Sulky, surly. "He's a grouty man."

growed   The past tense of *grew*, "They growed it in their garden."

grub hysen   An old term for sassafras tea; *hysan* is Chinese for "green tea."

gully-jumper   A derogatory name for a backwoodsman. *See* HILLBILLY; RIDGE RUNNER.

gully washer   A heavy rain; often one that doesn't fall for long but does much damage.

gum   1) A name for a rabbit trap in the Ozarks. Chewing gum there is called *wax*. 2) A beehive made of a hollow log section. 3) A well curb made from a hollow log section. 4) Pine tar. 5) To chew something without teeth, with the gums. "Ain't got teeth anymore. Haf to gum my terbacker." (Stuart, "Whose Land Is This?")

gut   Frequently a pronunciation of *got* in the Kentucky Cumberlands and elsewhere.

guvment   A pronunciation of *government*. "The guvment agents broke up his still."

haint 1) A ghost. "'And then we just rubbed the hell out of the horse chestnuts we carry to keep the haints at bay and put them in my baptismal cup and rattled them hard and coated the whole countryside in a cure that was half-Christian, half-savage. I tell you, boy, we put some powerful hoo-doo up in them mountains.'" (Middleton, *Spine of Time*) 2) Also means have not or has not. "He haint done it."

half-baked yokum A fool. "She's a half-baked yokum." *Yokum* is probably the origin of the Yokum family name in the long-popular comic strip *Lil Abner*.

half in two In halves, in two pieces. "They cut it half in two."

half-moon pie A pie shaped in a half-circle and usually filled with fried apples.

half-pint Baptists *See* FORTY-GAL-LON BAPTISTS.

half-runner bean A white firm pea bean very popular in the southern mountains.

ham-meat A pleonasm for ham. "Here is cold ham-meat." (Stuart, *Beyond Dark Hills*)

hammer's back See COCKED.

hand-going In succession. "I've had a headache two days hand-goin' now."

handily Honestly. "You can't handily blame him for what he did."

handsome Handsomely. "The big fellers that make lots of money . . . ought to pay handsome for it." (Kephart, *Southern Highlanders*)

handwrite Handwriting. "I know his handwrite like my own."

happy as a dead pig in the sunshine A colorful saying meaning very happy, its origin lost in time.

happy-pappies A term hillfolk use for men on welfare or men employed in makework projects.

h'ar *See* B'AR.

hard fight with a big stick A difficult task or job to perform. "Don't know if I should take it on—it's a hard fight with a big stick."

hardness Bad feelings, bad blood between people, especially families. "The hardness twixt them goes back to their grandfather." *See* RIGHT SMART OF HARDNESS.

hard oil Axle grease or any hard nonflowing oil used on farm equipment.

harelip To disfigure or destroy. "She's hell-bent to do it even if it harelips all the hogs in Tennessee."

harrycane A frequent pronunciation of hurricane in the Ozarks.

hast Has. "Time and hard work hast changed Ma . . ." (Stuart, *Trees of Heaven*)

hate A little bit, a small amount. "I don't give a hate about it." Sometimes seen as *hait*.

hateful 1) A term used in the southern Appalachians for anything very obnoxious. "Them bugs—the little old hatefuls!" (Kephart, *Southern Highlanders*) 2) A name for people who are mean, nasty and hateful. "Them Pea Ridge folk is all hatefuls."

Hatfield and McCoy feud A famous feud in the Kentucky mountains that began in 1878 with the theft of a hog by one of the families and eventually claimed 12 lives before it ended years later. The names have become synonymous nationally for any bitter family feud.

haul one's coat Take off one's coat for a whipping. "He made Pa haul his coat." (Stuart, *Men of the Mountains*)

have rabbit in one's feet To be restless, to wander about. "That man's had rabbit in his feet long as I remember."

have the big eye 1) To be greedy, desire material things. 2) To have insomia. "I had the big eye three nights running."

have you ever tried to separate fly shit from black pepper? Heard in Arkansas to describe any very difficult, painstaking, almost impossible task.

haw-eater 1) A derogatory name for a backwoodsman, implying all highlanders eat the bitter berries of the hawthorne tree. 2) A nickname for a West Virginian, because West Virginians were said to like to eat the berrylike fruit of the black hawthorne tree.

hawg A common pronunciation of hog, just as *dog* is pronounced *dawg*.

hawkbill A hooked or sharp nose. "He's noted for that hawkbill of his."

hay-shaker An insulting derogatory name for a mountaineer. *See* HILLBILLY; RIDGE RUNNER.

head A name for the poisonous copperhead snake (*Agkistrodon contortrix*); a shortening of *copperhead*.

heading   A pillow, so named from its place at the head of the bed. "Corn cobs make a pretty sorry headin'."

head of the heap   Used to describe the leader of any enterprise, from a group of boys to a business. "He's the head of the heap there and won't let you forget it."

heap a folks   An old English usage meaning a lot of people that is still used among highlanders. "There's a heap a folks a-comin'." Heap can also refer to a large amount of other things: "We-uns ate a heap of chicken."

heap right rather   Much rather. "I'd a heap right rather git a soon (early) start."

heap sight   Much. "I'd a heap sight rather stay home than go abroad." *See* ABROAD.

hear a fox bark in the night   Considered a bad omen by some hill people. "I knowed he died when I heard a fox bark in the night."

heared   Heard. "The sweetest prayers I ever heared pray was from the lips of my mother." (L. N. Roberts, *Cutshin and Greasy*).

heart   *See* TABOO WORDS.

hear tell   To hear or learn something said or spoken of. "You run 'im out 'n this country and we've never heard tell of 'im." (Jesse Stuart, "Grandpa Birdwell," 1941)

hearts-a-bustin'-with-love   The burning bush (*Euonymus americana*) which has seed pods that burst open to reveal many scarlet seeds. It also goes by the names *hearts-a-bustin'*, *strawberry bush*, *swamp dogwood*, *arrowwood* and *spindle bush*.

heifer   An Ozarkian term for a gossip or meddler, someone always chewing his or her cud.

heir   Used as a verb for *to inherit*. "He heired the house from his brother."

hell   Mountaineers in North Carolina and elsewhere give the name *hells* to the tangles of laurel and rhododendron that cover mile after mile of steep mountainsides. The term is first recorded in 1883 but is probably considerably older. Synonyms are *laurel licks*, *wooly heads*, *lettuce beds*, *yaller patches* and *blackberry hell*. Sometimes a person's name is attached to a particular hell, such as *Herman's hell*, in remembrance of somebody lost in the mazes of wild vegetation. "A 'hell' or 'slick' or 'wooly head' or 'yaller patch' is a thicket of land of rhododendron, impassable except where the bears have bored out trails." (Kephart, *Southern Highlanders*)

hell ain't a mile away and the fences all down   A colorful way to describe a terribly hot day in the Ozarks.

hellatious   Excellent, terrific. "I remember a dog he had one time named Suzie he said was a hellatious bird dog." (McCarthy, *Child of God*)

hell-fired A common intensive. "The Praths were hell-fired mad at Ceif." (Stuart, "Bury Your Dead")

hello, brother! An old-fashioned greeting once common in the Ozarks.

hell's banjoo (banjo) An old oath from the southern Appalachians. "Hell's banjoo if I ain't lost my folding knife." (Chapman, *Happy Mountain*)

hell's fuzzy! A common exclamation similar to the widespread *hell's bells!*

helt Held. "We jist helt hands." (Jesse Stuart, "When Foxes Flirt," 1938)

hen fruit A humorous term for eggs in the Ozarks and southern Appalachians. "We were liven' off hen fruit for a time there."

hen-wood Legend has it that the mountain tree hen-wood (*Bumelia lanuginosa*), also called *chittamwood*, was the wood used to build Noah's Ark.

hep A pronunciation of *help*. "'Can I hep ye, son?' he said." (McCarthy, *Orchard Keeper*)

her Herself. "She bought her a dress for the party."

hern Hers. An old English poem goes: She that prigs (steals) what isn't hern, / At the treadmill takes a turn." *See* HIS'N and the INTRODUCTION.

he's (she's) folks He's okay, all right, a regular guy.

hesh Hush. "Hesh up your cryin', child."

het Past tense of heat. "He het it up good."

hiat Hoist. "Hiat that rope up there."

hid away Put away. "Get them toys hid away, company's comin'."

high as a Georgia pine Very drunk. "He's high as a Georgia pine and keeps on growin'."

high as the hair on a cat's back Very expensive; a common term in the Ozarks.

high blood High blood pressure; *low blood* means low blood pressure. "The doc's treatin' me fer high blood."

high lonesome Said in the Ozarks of someone drinking heavily while alone. "He went on a high lonesome."

hillbilly This derogatory name for a hill person is considered insulting, at best, and has in the past provoked fights resulting in deaths. It is first recorded in 1904 and implies laziness, ignorance and stupidity. Highlanders don't mind being called hillbillies by other mountain folk, but they do object to FLATLANDERs or FURRINERs using the term. *See* HAW-EATER; RIDGE RUNNER.

hill-hawk An insulting term used in the central Pennsylvania mountains for a lazy shiftless mountain resident. *See* HILLBILLY.

hinder Used in the central Pennsylvania mountains for the fundament or backside.

hindsight before Backwards. "You put your sweater on hindside before." Also *hindside first.*

hippin A baby's diaper. "The boy needs a clean hippin." Said to derive from *hip.*

hippoed Suffering from an imaginary ailment, the word deriving from *hypochondria.* "There goes that pore hippoed woman."

hip-shot Badly injured, disabled. "He was hip-shot in that fray with the Coles."

his (her) backbone's rubbin' his (her) belly He or she is very hungry, starving.

his (her) head's not done He or she is not very intelligent. "Tom's head ain't done."

his'n A contraction of "his own." Though heard in the Southern mountains, it is not as generally thought to be a backwoods Americanism, but a word of long and respectable lineage. It dates back to the early 15 century and was used by Samuel Richardson in his novel *Clarissa* (1747). An old English adage goes "Him as prigs (steals) what isn't his'n / When he's cotched he goes to prison." *See* HERN; HOUSEN.

hisself Often used for *himself* by highlanders, as in "He got hisself some vittles."

hissy fit A hysterical fit thrown by a very disturbed and angry person. *Hissy* here may derive from *hysterical.* Also heard as *throw a hissy* and *pitch a hissy.*

hit A frequent pronunciation of *it* by mountain folk, usually at the beginning of a sentence for emphasis, as in "hit's too soon for that." Though considered illiterate today, *hit* derives from the Anglo-Saxon *hit,* the neuter of *he,* which was standard English until at least the 12th century.

hitch-up An old term in the Ozarks and elsewhere meaning to marry. "They got hitched-up last month."

hit's It's. Sometimes *it* is used to refer to a child, taking the place of *he* or *she,* as in "Hit's a good child and haint nary bit of trouble to me." (L. N. Roberts, *Cutshin and Greasy*)

hit some people with a sour apple and they got drunk as a biled (boiled) owl A folk saying from the Ozarks about people who can't hold their moonshine.

hit the grit To start out, begin a journey, hit the road. "Well it's about time to hit the grit." The *grit* in the expression probably refers to a gravel road.

hoe Sometimes used in the Ozarks to mean *hose, stockings.* "There's a hole in your hoe." (Katrina Johnson, *Evening Street*, 1947)

hoe handle A euphemism for the penis, as is *long tool.*

hog-and-panther To pester, henpeck, "She hog-and-panthered him till he had to take her . . ." (Wilson, *Backwoods America*)

hog-killing time A most enjoyable time, a lively celebration; after the parties customarily held when hogs where slaughtered.

hog-leg A long-barreled pistol. "I always pack my hog-leg."

hog meat An old-fashioned term for pork in the Ozarks.

hog-ranger Another insulting derogatory name for a mountaineer. *See* HILLBILLY.

hog-tight, bull-strong and horse-high Used to describe a well-built, strong structure, especially a fence.

hog-wild Very excited. "Gardner's mule had gone hog-wild." (Wright, *Shepherd*)

hold your tater (potato) Calm down, be patient. "Hold your tater for another half hour." (Stuart, *Beyond Dark Hills*)

holler 1) A hollow, a valley, usually narrow with a stream of water running through it. "He lives in an awful bad holler." (Stuart, "Uncle Joe's Boys") 2) A word often used in place names, such as Possum Holler.

hollered like whores at a camp meeting An old saying dating back to mid-19th-century America.

holler up To wake someone up by shouting his name. "Holler me up by six so I can get to work."

holp The past tense of *help.* "She holp him do all his chores."

holt Hold. "'Now, Spring,' he quavered, 'you got to get holt of yourself.'" (Kantor, *Bugle Ann*)

home boy Used in the Ozarks and South, for somebody from one's hometown or area; the expression is now used in many U.S. urban areas as well.

home-folks One's immediate family. "All my home-folks were together for the first time in years."

hone To long for. "I hone for her every day." The word derives from the Middle French *hoigner*, meaning to long for.

hone off In the Ozarks, to have sexual intercourse. "He honed her off."

honey Once commonly heard as a term of friendship among men in the southern Appalachians, much like *partner* or *buddy.*

honey fuggle Used in the central Pennsylvania mountains for flatter or cajole.

honey hole A huge hold dug in mountain coal towns to hold the excrement from the town's privies. During the Great Depression one group of miners held a mock-burial in a honey hole of President Herbert Hoover, on whom they blamed the bad times. A wooden slab prominently displayed his mock-epitaph:

HERE LIES HOOVER,
DAMN HIS SOUL,
BURIED IN A HONEY HOLE.
LET HIM LAY HERE TILL
   THE END,
POOR MAN'S ENEMY,
RICH MAN'S FRIEND.

honey pond and flitter tree An expression used in the Ozarks and southern Appalachians to indicate a life full of good things. "They found the honey pond and flitter tree."

honey wine *See* METHINGLUM.

hongry A pronunciation of *hungry*. Also heard as *hawngry* in the Ozarks. "I hate to kill anything when it's hongry." (Lealon Jones, *Swappin' Fever*, 1939)

hoodoo Magic. *See* quote under HAINT.

hoorah Hurry. "Hoorah there and get finished with your chores."

hoot A drink. "You give me two hoots of corn licker." (Stuart, *Beyond Dark Hills*)

hootenanny 1) A darn, as in "I don't give a hootenanny!" 2) An informal performance by folksingers. Origin unknown.

hoot-n-holler A short distance. "It's just a hoot-n-holler from here."

hope how soon I'll see you I hope I'll see you soon.

horn Used by Ozarkians as a synonym for *penis*, but not in polite company.

horn-bugle A pleonasm for *bugle*. "He can really play that horn-bugle."

horny *See* PRUNEY.

horseback The rider of a horse in the Ozarks is sometimes called a *horseback*.

horsebit To be bitten by a horse. "He was horsebit by that mean stallion."

horse dose Medicine given in large quantity. "Doc gave him a horse dose of penicillin."

horse-quart An oversize quart of something. "I pulled a horse-quart of moonshine from my saddlebags." (Stuart, *Men of the Mountains*)

horse-throwed Said of someone thrown by a horse. "Ike Morgan Pringle's been a-horse-throwed down the cliff." (Kephart, *Southern Highlanders*)

hot as a red beet Sexually excited. "She makes him hot as a red beet."

hotten Heat up, warm. "Let me hotten your coffee."

hotter'n a two-dollar pistol Very hot, an allusion to cheap 19th-century pistols that got hot when fired.

hot-toe-mitty An exclamation of surprise or wonderment. "It was an older man came to the door . . . 'Hot-toe-mitty,' he said, slow and evenly. Then: 'Well come on in if you're able. They entered, the [wounded] man hobbling on his pole and the boy following." (McCarthy, *Orchard Keeper*)

hound See quote. "[It] was the custom [among hunters] never to refer to a fox-hound as a 'dog.' They were all 'hounds.'" (Kantor, *Bugle Ann*)

hound dog A hound or dog. "It was like carryin' a full-grown hound-dog pup to carry the fox." (Stuart, *Men of the Mountains*) The expression is known nationally today, due in large part to Elvis Presley's rendition of "You Ain't Nothin' But a Hound Dog."

hour by sun Before sunset or after sunrise. "It's an hour by sun."

house Sometimes used for the largest room in the house, the living room or the kitchen. "It's too hot here, we better sit in the house."

housen Chaucer used the n-stem, or weak declension, in words like *housen*, for house, and *treen*, for trees, long before the hillfolk; in fact the standard English nouns *children* and *oxen* still retain this form.

house plunder An old term for household furnishings.

how does your tobacker (tobacco) taste today? A greeting among hillfolk meaning "How are you, how are you feeling today?"

howdy How do you do. "We spoke howdy and traded small talk." (Wilson, *Backwoods America*) The most common greeting in the Ozarks.

howms Swampy places, mud flats. "You can't bring a horse through those howms."

huckleberry pie The best, excellent. "Life has been all huckleberry pie this year."

huge-big A pleonasm for *huge*. "He was a huge-big man."

hug-me-tight A type of small wagon into which two people fit snugly. "I've seen this road filled with surreys, buggies, joltwagons and hug-me-tights." (Stuart, "Whose Land Is This?")

hull Whole. "I want the hull amount right now."

hull-gull A game played with small stones, round nuts or marbles in which one player conceals a number of such objects in his closed fist, his opponent trying to guess how many objects he is hiding.

human rifle An old large-caliber rifle powerful enough to kill people rather than small game.

hunting Looking for. "'Mr. Gibson's huntin' you,' the man said." (McCarthy, *Child of God*)

hurd The past tense of hear. "We hurd it before you did."

hurt Harm. "He never done no hurt to one of God's critters." (Movie version of Wright's *The Shepherd of the Hills*)

hurted Hurt. "He got hurted real bad."

husband-high Said in the Ozarks of a young woman considered old enough to be married.

hush your mouthing Shut up. "'All right, boys,' says Bad-Eye, 'hush your mouthing. I've got my pistol up.'" (Jesse Stuart, "Not Without Guns," 1939)

hyar A pronunciation of *hear*, with a *y* added in place of the *e*.

hystericky A way Ozark hill people say *hysterical*. "All the crowd was hystericky."

I ain't a-hurting for you I don't need you. "Leave me if you will; I ain't a-hurting for you."

I ain't much of a fool about I'm not fond of. "I ain't much of a fool about them snaps (green beans)."

I ain't never done no dirt of no kind to nobody. An example of a quintuple negative from a region where double negatives, triple negatives, etc., are commonplace.

I'd druther A pronunciation of *I'd rather*. "I'd druther go with John than with Pa."

idjit A pronunciation of *idiot*. "Git that idjit out of here."

idlesome Lazy, slothful, unambitious. "Martha never used to be so idlesome."

I done it Frequently used for "I did it" in the Ozarks.

I don't care to do it Heard among hillfolk for "I have no objection to doing it," or "I don't mind doing it."

I don't chaw my terbacker but once. I don't say something more than once, don't repeat myself.

I'd sooner sleep in the pasture and pick corn out of horsedroppings. I'd rather do almost anything else than what you propose.

I'd take it kindly. I'd really appreciate it. "I'd take it kindly if you'd loan me some short-sweetening (sugar)."

idy Idea. "She's got no idy how it's done." Also, *idee*.

iffen If "Iffen he comes, I leave."

if I had my rathers If I had my choice. "If I had my rathers, I'd choose that one." Based on *I'd rather have*.

I generally surround it. I usually go around it. "I generally surround that swamp when I go that way."

I-God! A common exclamation. "I-God what a fire!" Also *y-God, Aye God*.

I gonnies! A euphemistic exclamation, a variation of *My God!* used in the Ozarks and southern Appalachians. "I gonnies he was a big man!"

71

ill Ill-tempered, cross, nasty, vicious. "The older dog don't generally raise no ruction; hit's the younger one that's ill." (Kephart, *Southern Highlanders*)

I'll be dogged! An old-fashioned exclamation of surprise.

I'll declare. A common exclamation. "I'll declare I thought she had the prettiest teeth." (Stuart, *Men of the Mountain*)

I'll eat the goose that fattens on your grave. I'll outlive you by many years.

I'll tell you why I done it fer. I'll tell you why I did it.

I loved the sweat of his body and the dust of his feet more than any other man. The poetic words of an old mountain woman recalling the extent of her love for her husband, who had died many years before.

I'm a curly-tailed wolf with a pink ass and this is my night to howl! A humorous oath heard among drinkers of potent moonshine.

I'm tellin' you right I'm telling you the truth. "'Oh, Lord, I'm tellin' you right, I'd like to live my life over.'" (R. E. Thomas, *Come Go With Me*)

indeed an in-double-deed Often used for emphasis, as in "Indeed an in-double-deed I won't do it!"

infare A celebration or reception after a wedding. Also called a *serenade*, a *shivaree*, *enfare* and *onfare*.

in good heart In good spirits, good health. "He's been in good heart since she came back to him."

inkle Inkling, bit, hint. "I haven't got an inkle what's in his mind."

in reason Logically. "I knowed in reason she'd be upset."

in the gales In a good state of mind, good humor, very cheerful. "Pa's in the gales; it's a good time to ask him."

in time At one time. "Somebody had tapped the maple trees in time."

irk Weary. "He came many an irk mile down from the mountains carrying the wounded boy in his arms."

isabel Still heard in the central Pennsylvania mountains in relatively recent times for a brownish-yellow, light dun or cream-colored horse. An old story, which may be just that, has it that the color isabel is named for the underwear of the Archduchess Isabella of Austria. It seems that Isabella vowed never to change her underwear until her husband the Archduke Albert captured the city of Ostend. This effort took three years, until 1604, and Isabella's underwear must have looked *isabel* or *isabelline* by then.

I swan! *See* SWAN.

it makes hell look like a lightnin' bug A description of any big fire.

I wouldn't have her (him) if her (his) head was strung with gold. A colorful way to describe the rejection of a suitor.

jag A small pile. "I reckon I better be cuttin' you-all a little jag of wood this morning." (William R. Lighton, *Happy Hollow Farm*, 1915)

jailhouse fish Fish that is caught out of season; if the game warden catches you catching such fish you can wind up in the jailhouse.

jake leg 1) The d.t.'s, delirium tremens, caused by bad liquor. 2) A paralysis or partial paralysis caused by bad liquor. "I never saw so many men walkin' on canes with the jake leg." (Stuart, *Trees of Heaven*)

jakey Old-fashioned or countrified. "She wore all those jakey dresses."

jam-rock A side stone in a fireplace. "She struck [her pipe] on the jam-rock above the fireplace." (Stuart, *Men of the Mountains*)

janders A frequent pronunciation of *jaundice* in the Ozarks. "He was yellow with janders."

jape 1) An old term for *copulate*. 2) To seduce or take advantage of.

jar fly A common name for the cicada.

jedge A frequent pronunciation of *judge*; heard in other regions as well.

jemison This old, probably obsolete, term for the penis possibly takes its name from the poisonous jimsonweed plant, once regarded as an aphrodisiac.

jibble up Cut up into little pieces. "She jibbled up the beans before she cooked them."

jig A small amount. "I sold him a jig of firewood."

jill-flirt Someone who breaks wind often and noisily; origin unknown. *See* DON'T AMOUNT TO A POOT IN A WINDSTORM.

jillikens An old term for the far backwoods. "They live deep in the jillikens."

jim-kay A historical term meaning to stuff with food to a dangerous point. According to one story, a family kept a pet pig that they named James K. Polk, after the U.S. president, and fed James (or Jim) K. so much that he burst apart. Thus the President's name became the basis for this odd word.

jimmey Slip around. "The pipe jimmeys in Fromme's mouth because several of her front teeth are out and it is hard for her to hold the pipestem." (Stuart, *Trees of Heaven*)

jimmy jawed Said of someone with a prominent projecting lower jaw.

jimplicute An imaginary monster shaped like a dragon once believed to haunt the roads and fields at night.

jined A common pronunciation of *joined* that dates back to 18th-century England, as witness this rhyming couplet in Alexander Pope's *Essay on Man* (1732): In praise so just let every man be jined / And fill the general chorus of mankind.

jingleberries A synonym for *testicles* among highlanders.

jist A pronunciation of *just*, "He jist got here." Also *jest*.

jist a little piece A short distance. "The store's jist a little piece down the road."

job of work A redundancy for job or work. "I'd take any job of work to feed us."

joe To move slowly. "He joed along the path." The word's origin is unknown, but it might derive from

the name of someone named Joe who was lazy.

joe-darter Someone or something unsurpassed, the best. "That's a joe-darter of a gun." Origin unknown.

jokey Given to practical jokes, fun loving. "He's a jokey fellow."

jolt-wagon A rude, old-fashioned wagon without springs that jolts passengers as it moves along.

joree bird Another name in the mountains for the towhee or chewink.

jower To argue. "They were jowerin' about it all night."

joy o' the mountain A more colorful name for the trailing arbutus.

juba To leap wildly about. "He made them dance juba."

judge Can mean a fool or a clown in the Ozarks as well as an officer of the law. Often pronounced *jedge* to rhyme with *hedge*.

juice A common term for electricity. "They're so far back in the woods they got no juice."

jump the broom with Marry. "He jumped the broom with her years ago." The phrase derives from the ancient practice, once legal in many places, of broomstick marriages, when couples only had to jump over a broomstick held by two people to be declared man and wife.

jumpy as a pregnant fox in a forest fire Very nervous, anxious, distraught.

just a small, puny, little old thing A colorful way of describing someone or something very small. "He's just a small, puny, little old thing."

just got a bound to Have to be, must. "We've just got a bound to be neighborly." (J. Thomas, *Blue Ridge Country*)

katynipper Another name for the dragonfly.

keep close to the willows Be modest, conservative. Said to derive from the practice of boys who swam in the nude keeping close to the concealing willow trees lining the creek.

keep your dobbers up Be courageous, screw up your courage.

keep your tail in the water Keep calm; said to derive from the practice of hill men calming excited horses by leading them into water up to their tails.

keer A pronunciation of *care*. "I don't keer what he does."

Kentuck screamer Historical term for a Kentuckian. "'I say you old Kentuck screamer, what kind o' livin' had you while you were up the stream?'" (Henry Wetson, *Nights in a Block House*, 1852)

Kentucky fire Still another colorful name for potent MOONSHINE.

Kentucky rifle Famous in American history as the rifle of the pioneers, the long, extremely accurate Kentucky rifle is recorded by this name as early as 1838. The flintlock muzzle loader should, however, be called the *Pennsylvania rifle*, for it was first made in that state by Swiss gunmakers in the 1730s and was perfected there. "The British bayonet was no match for the Kentucky rifle," wrote one early chronicler.

Kentucky right turn William Safire's "On Language" column in the *New York Times* (January 27, 1991) notes this as a humorous term meaning "the maneuver performed when a driver, about to turn right, first swings to the left."

Kentucky windage A method of correcting the sighting of a rifle by aiming the weapon to one side of the target instead of adjusting the sights. A practice of mountain men sharpshooters.

Kentucky yell "A still louder laugh presently increased into a Kentucky yell." (Solomon Smith, *The Theatrical Apprenticeship of Solomon Smith*, 1846)

ketch The usual pronunciation of *catch* among highlanders.

ketched Pregnant. The word is not usually spoken in the presence of women.

ketchy weather Weather that is unsettled, that is unpredictable. "The weather was very ketchy this year."

kick the cat To become angry. "Widdie Washburn kicked the cat. She acted mad because we'd come." (Jesse Stuart, "When Foxes Flirt," 1938)

kilfliggin An old-fashioned term for *lazy*, its origin unknown. "He's a kilfliggin man."

kill-devil Potent moonshine so poorly made that it could kill the devil himself.

kill your own snakes Mind your own business. A variation is *cut your own weeds*.

kilt Killed. "I've kilt a many a squirrel in that tree." (Stuart, *Trees of Heaven*) *See* SALAT.

kilted An old central Pennsylvania mountain term meaning "tucked up in bed."

kindly Kind of, sort of. "Going up the hollow was kindly like going up a big, green tunnel." (Stuart, *Men of the Mountains*)

kinfolks Relatives, kinfolks. "For two hundred years the Robertson 'kinfolks' have inhabited the foothills of the Blue Ridge." (*Time*, 9/28/42) *See* HOME-FOLKS.

King's Mountain Day October 7, the anniversary of the day in 1780 when 900 "mountain men" defeated a much larger British force at King's Mountain, South Carolina.

kitchen-settin' weather Weather in early fall when it starts getting chilly and folks sit around the kitchen range or fireplace.

kiver A common pronunciation of *cover*. "Kiver your baby up in this cold."

kivered cars An old term for a railroad train. "He took the kivered cars to the city."

knee-deep in summer In the middle of summer.

knee-high to a jack rabbit Very small.

knitting pain A stitch or cramp in the side. "I was bent over from a knitting pain."

knockers The testicles. Pig's testicles, believed to be an aphrodisiac by some, are sold as *pig's knockers*.

knowance Knowledge. "She had knowance of his cheatin' ways."

knowed Knew. "She said: 'I knowed you'd do me thisaway.'" (McCarthy, *Child of God*)

knowings Knowledge. "Not to my knowings." (Stuart, *Men of the Mountains*)

know in reason Know with certainty. "She knew in reason he would be there."

koosy Outdated, tacky, unfashionable, especially as concerns women's clothing. "That's a koosy dress she's wearin'."

laid off Doesn't mean "dismissed from a job" in mountain country, but means "planned to," as in "I've been layin' off to ketch me some fish," or "He laid off to visit me but his car broke down."

lamp-lifting time An old, probably obsolete, Ozarkian term for dusk. Also called *candle-light.*

Land of Blood A nickname for Kentucky since the early 19th century, when it was famous for its Indian wars.

Land of the Sky A nickname, since at least the turn of the century, for the Great Smoky Mountains region in North Carolina.

lap Wrap. "He lapped up the baby in a blanket.

larripin' good Very good, delicious. "Them's larripin' good peas."

lashings and lavins Plenty, lots of. "They've got lashings and lav-ins of money." Originally an Anglo-Irish term.

'lasses Molasses. "And they had been some other fellers that made 'lasses that thought they was good, too." (R. E. Thomas, *Come Go With Me*)

lasty Long lasting, durable. "It's lasty clothes she makes for the children."

lath-open bread See quote. "[A bread] made from biscuit dough, with soda and buttermilk, in the usual way, except that the shortening is worked in last . . . baked in flat cakes, parting readily into thin flakes when broken edgewise. I suppose that [the term] denotes that it opens into lathlike strips." (Kephart, *Southern Highlanders*)

laurel slick *See* HELL.

laurely Covered with laurel. "That side of the mountain is powerful steep and laurely."

lavish 1) Often means a large number of something, as in "He had a lavish of melons." 2) Plenty. "If anyone wanted a history of this country . . . he'd git a lavish of it by reading that mine-suit testimony." (Kephart, *Southern Highlanders*)

lawed Litigated, went to court to establish rights, sued. "They lawed fer that piece of land." (L. N. Roberts, *Cutshin and Greasy*)

Law, I reckon! Lord I reckon; a common southern Appalachian exclamation.

Law me! Lordy me! Another exclamation often heard in the southern Appalachians.

Laws a mercy! Lord of mercy; still another common southern Appalachian exclamation.

lay back To save, save up. "Ma will lay back a few pennies from every dozen of eggs she sells." (Stuart, *Trees of Heaven*)

laying the worm See quote. "'Well, generally, they would make a feller some rails and lay them out where he wanted to build the fence. That's called *laying the worm*.'" (R. E. Thomas, *Come Go With Me*)

layin' off Putting off, postponing. "I been layin' off payin' those taxes."

laylock The way mountaineers say *lilac* in the Ozarks.

lay off *See* LAID OFF.

layover to catch meddlers An evasive answer usually given to curious or prying children, "That's a layover to catch meddlers." A layover is a bear-trap consisting of a pit covered with branches, a deadfall.

lean toward Jesus A carpenter's expression for something slanted, out of plumb.

least 1) Smallest. "They won't be jumping on the least man on Whetstone." (Stuart, "Not Without Guns") 2) Youngest. "Her least girl is a big help to her."

leastways At least. "Leastways we have a few dollars saved for food."

leather breeches See quote. "Beans dried in the pod, then boiled 'hull and all' are called leather breeches [this is not slang but the regular name]." (Kephart, *Southern Highlanders*)

leftment A fragment. "He put all the leftments of bread before his guest." (Chapman, *Happy Mountain*)

left out Left. "He left out fer home an hour ago."

less Smaller. "Don't hit someone less than you."

let go Say, give as an estimate. "The road's back yonder, let go about a mile."

lettuce beds *See* HELL.

license Sometimes used as the plural. "Why I says to the man, 'I want some license.'" (Stuart, "Uncle Joe's Boys")

licker Liquor. "That's right good licker."

lickety-whoop Fast, quickly, a synonym for the more common *lickety-split*. "He passed him lickety-whoop down the hill."

lids The covers or boards of a book. "You'll find the answer between the lids of this book."

lief Mountain speech sometimes still employs the old form *lief* (prefer), in *as* constructions like "I 'ud as lief to shoot the sorry old critter as no."

lie tale A malicious story that is a complete lie told seriously and intended to defame someone. "That's a lie tale she told, Luke, don't listen to it."

light Alight. "Light from your horse and visit awhile."

light a rag To leave in a hurry. "He lit a rag for home." (Kephart, *Southern Highlanders*)

light a shuck To leave hastily. "As soon as he saw Big John coming, he lit a shuck for the big timber."

light-bread Store-bought, commercial bread as opposed to home-baked white bread.

lightning bug A firefly.

light out like a scalded dog To clear out quickly, often running away, like a dog someone throws scalding water on. "Billy lit out like a scalded dog."

like A pronunciation of *lack* in the Ozarks. "He liked ten cents to buy the candy."

like climbin' a ground pole with two baskets of eggs To attempt or perform a very difficult, involved task.

like for To like, the *for* redundant. "I'd like for you to go ahead." (Stuart, *Beyond Dark Hills*)

likely Probably. "This is likely the last season we'll have up here together."

like poundin' sand in a rat hole To perform a very easy task. "He couldn't pound sand in a rat note."

limb To whip or beat. "He limbed the boy bad."

line out To line up, organize. "My mind was in a muddle. If ever I could get lined out just right, I'd show them I wasn't a fake." (Stuart, *Beyond Dark Hills*)

lines Another word for reins. "Don't pull on her lines too hard."

linguister Heard in the southern Appalachians for an interpreter.

literary school An old-fashioned term for a public school where only academic subjects are taught, not a religious school or a music school, for example. "She went to the literary school eight years."

little jag   *See* JAG

lived over it   Endured something, made the best of circumstances. "'Daddy [was strict] . . . But I've lived over it. I had my ninety-fifth birthday last June.'" (R. E. Thomas, *Come Go With Me*)

live with the world   To concern oneself only with material things, to live one's life with no thought of spiritual matters.

loaferin' about   *See*   COOTERIN' AROUND.

lonesome   Lonesomely.   "The wind kindly blowed lonesome." (Stuart, *Men of the Mountains*)

lonesome water   Sweet water from close to one's first home. "I knowed you'd come back to drink of lonesome water. Once you get a drink of lonesome water you always come home." (Jesse Stuart, *Beyond Dark Hills*, 1938)

long ever ago   A long time ago. "Long ever ago I promised him I would jump the broom (get married)."

long handles   Long johns, long underwear. "He wears them long handles winter and summer."

long potato   Another name for a sweet potato, which is generally longer than a white potato.

long shot with a limb in the way Bad odds, a chancy proposition. "He might win, but it's a long shot with a limb in the way."

long sweetening   Molasses, honey or syrup. *See* SHORT SWEETENING.

long-tongue   A gossip or tale bearer. "Don't listen to that long-tongue about anything."

long tool   *See* HOE HANDLE.

looby   Heard in the Ozarks for a clumsy, dull man or woman.

lookahere   Look over here. "'Hey,' they said. 'Lookahere. It's the Ridge Runner . . .'" (Meredith Sue Willis, *In the Mountains of America*, 1994) *See* RIDGE RUNNER.

looking porely   Having a sick appearance or being ill. "He's been lookin' porely a year now."

loose as a goose   To have diarrhea. "I was loose as a goose down in Mexico."

Lord help my time!   A common Appalachian exclamation.

Lord's eye on it   No doubt of it, without a doubt, certainly. "'[That's] true, brother. Lord's eye on it.'" (Middleton, *Spine of Time*)

losel A good-for-nothing. "She's been goin' with that losel Jake Helms."

louse around To loiter, waste time, loaf. "He's been lousin' around all winter."

loud Having a strong or bad smell. "I love that loud sweet smell." (Stuart, *Trees of Heaven*)

love apple A term for the tomato that is common in other languages and was once popular in the Ozarks. The tomato was long held to be a powerful aphrodisiac.

love-hole Heard in the Ozarks for a gully, ditch or depression along a road. Such a gully often caused a female passenger in a buggy or car to bump up against the male driver or jolted the two riders into one another's arms.

low Short. "She's a low woman, he looks twice as tall." *Also see* ALLOW.

low and little with it Describes a short, thin person, as in "He's low and little with it."

low blood *See* HIGH BLOOD.

lowlands The flatlands, as opposed to the mountains or hills.

low-rate To put down, criticize in a malicious manner. "He better stop low-ratin' me or I'll fist him good one day."

low wine A low-proof moonshine. "Dont't give me none of that low wine."

lumpus In a heap. "She fainted and fell down lumpus."

lusty Once common in the central Pennsylvania mountains for beautiful, pleasant, cheerful, with no indication of its usual meaning.

lying out *See* SHUN OUT.

mad as all get-out   Extremely mad. *See* ALL GET-OUT.

madder 'n a wet hen   Very mad indeed; now widespread in use. "Maggie was madder 'n a wet hen when she saw her man with Doris."

mad-doctor   An old term for a psychiatrist that is seldom heard anymore.

mah   A pronunciation of *my*. "That's mah brother over there."

maiden   *See* TABOO WORDS.

main big   Very big. "That main big old dog worried him."

main holt (hold)   Favorite pastime. "Fishing is his main holt."

make   A woman's figure. "She has a purty make and you can see it all in that dress she's wearin'."

make a branch   A euphemism for urinate. "He went outside to make a branch." *Branch* is a synonym for a stream or creek.

make a fancy   To win someone's favor, make a good impression on someone. "She's bent on makin' a fancy with Bobby Joe at the big dance."

make yourself pleasant   Make yourself at home. "Make yourself pleasant until I get done with these dishes." Also *make yourself pleased*.

making   Distilling moonshine. "He's been makin' shine thirty years now."

makin' more noise than a mule in a tin barn   Very noisy, suggested by an angry mule kicking the metal sides of a barn.

male brute   A euphemism for a bull. "A bull or boar is not to be mentioned as seen in mixed company, but male brute and hog are used as euphemisms." (Kephart, *Southern Highlanders*)

male-child   A male baby in the Ozarks. "They bought that little man-child all the play-pretties (toys) in the world."

mallyhack   To cut someone badly in a knife fight, wound him severely many times. "He mallyhacked Jed so bad he nearly killed him."

Man Above, The   A reverent name for God. "The Man Above watches over us."

mannerable   Good mannered, polite, a gentleman. "Even a mannerable man has his bad moments."

man-person   A man, just as *woman-person* and *gal-person* mean a woman.

manpower   Move by muscle alone. "He manpowered that tree off the road."

many a time   A great number of times. "I've rid this train a many a time." (Stuart, *Trees of Heaven*)

maple-head   Eponymous words and phrases often derive from the names of obscure people. This unusual old term from the Ozarks means "a very small head." It is said to come from a pioneer family named Maples noted for their small heads.

marrying close to home   The practice of people marrying their third, second and even first cousins.

marry up   Marry. "They're gonna marry up soon."

martin storm   The name for a spring storm occurring at about the time the martins return from the south.

marvels   An Ozark pronunciation of *marbles.*

mast   The season crop of nuts and acorns that is found on the forest floor and provides food for many animals. "Bears in the Smokies dine for days on end on mast."

master   The biggest, the best. "That's the master horse in these hills."

master onset   A great conflict or struggle. "There was a master onset between the two families that lasted years."

mater   Tomato; also heard as *tormater. See* LOVE APPLE.

maw   The common term for *mother*, though *mammy* and *mam* are also much used.

may   Might. "That church-house may've been standin' yet if the boys hadn't fixed it one night." (Stuart, "Whose Land Is This?")

mean as garbroth   Poor or inferior. *See* GARBROTH.

measly old smidgen   A very small piece. "Hain't et but a measly old smidgen of that pie."

meat   Sometimes used as a verb meaning to feed or supply with food. "That bear'll meat me a month." (Kephart, *Southern Highlanders*)

meetin'   Church services. "Are you going to Sunday meetin'?"

Melungeon The name of a people said to be of mixed white, black and American Indian ancestry living in the mountains of east Tennessee and west North Carolina.

memorize Remember. "I haint seen my sister in twenty years. I can't hardly memorize her." (Raine, "Land of Saddle Bags")

mend the fire Add wood to the fire, build it up before it goes out.

menfolks The males of a family. *See* SPEAR-SIDE.

mess Food enough for a meal. "I've et many a good mess of coon there." (Stuart, "Whose Land Is This?")

methinglum An old name for honey wine, commonly said to "kiss like a woman and kick like a mule."

mickety tuck A variation on *lickety-split*, very quickly.

midlin meat A mountain dish also known as *hog's jowl*.

might could Might be able to. "I might could fix that for you."

mighty Very. "They're mighty clever folks."

mimic A likeness. "That photograph's a fair mimic of him."

mincy Fastidiousness in one's eating habits. "[He's] mincy about

eating." (Kephart, *Southern Highlanders*)

mind To like. A mountaineer might say "I didn't mind it a bit," meaning he was terrified at looking over a precipice.

minner A minnow. "Little minners were playing." (Stuart, "When Hen Crows")

miration Surprise or wonder. Also pronounced *admiration*.

misdoubt To distrust or suspect. "I sure misdoubt him."

misery A pain. "She has a misery in her leg."

miseryn' Suffering. "She is just a-layin' there miseryn'."

misling Some hillfolk still refer to cool, foggy or misty weather as *misling*, just as Englishmen did seven centuries ago.

misput 1) Put out, annoyed. "I'm misput he said that about me." 2) Misplaced. "He misput his book."

misremember Forget. "He misremembered where he put it."

misorderly Disorderly. "The men are put up in the Greenup crib for misorderly conduct." (Stuart, *Beyond Dark Hills*)

Missouri Usually pronounced *Mizzoura* not *Miss-sou-ry*, by natives.

mistook Mistaken. "I was mistook about him—he's really a nice feller."

mistress Still used formally for one's wife among some hillfolk, as in "This is my mistress." Never used to mean "a kept woman."

mizzle A drizzle, a very light rain shower.

Mizzoura *See* MISSOURI.

moaningestfullest Mountain folk love to use comparative and superlative suffixes, which can be attached to any part of speech, as in "He was the moaningestfullest hound I ever did see." *Beautifulest, curiousest* and *workingest* are also good examples.

modesty songs Songs without ribald or bawdy or brash lyrics, of which there are many in the mountains.

molasseses *See* BAKING POWDERS.

mold warp See quote. "A mold warp is a slack-twisted, worthless man; a downgone wastrel." (Chapman, *Happy Mountain*)

mollyjoggers The name for a small fish (*Hypentelium nigricans*) common in the James River and elsewhere. The origin is unknown.

mommick See quote. "If a house be in disorder it is said to be all gormed or gaumed up, or things are just in a mommick." (Kephart, *Southern Highlanders*)

monkey *See* TWITCHET.

monkey-stove An old stove ordered from Montgomery Ward, a defunct catalog store which was once popularly called *Monkey Wards*.

moonrise The rising of the moon. "I'll be gone at moonrise." Also *moonup*.

moonshine Moonshine for illegally made whiskey wasn't coined in the hills, as one would guess, but probably originated in England and referred to a colorless brandy smuggled from France in the late 18th century. But a lot of moonshining still goes on in the mountains of Kentucky and Tennessee, where the product goes by many names recorded in these pages.

moonshine wars A name for the hostilities between moonshiners and Federal Prohibition agents during the Prohibition era, from 1920 to 1933. Hundreds of agents and moonshiners were killed in these "wars" and just one small group of agents is said to have destroyed a still every day for a year. *See* MOONSHINE.

moosey *See* TWITCHET.

more Often used in comparatives such as *more beautifuller, more hotter, more lonesomer, more meaner, more messier*, etc.

more pretty Prettier. "Lyn's more pretty than all of them girls."

mornglom Morning twilight, an hour before full dawn.

mort A great number. "A mort of things have to be decided."

mother naked Completely naked, naked as the day she or he was born to her or his mother.

mother wit Native intelligence, common sense as opposed to education or "book larnin'." "The man had no mother wit about him."

mought A common pronunciation of *might* in the Southern Appalachians. *See* quote under DRAP OFF.

mountain boomer 1) See quote. "Out of a tree overhead hopped a mountain 'boomer' [red squirrel]." (Kephart, *Southern Highlanders*) 2) A large collared lizard. *See* BOOMER; MOUNTAINEER.

mountain citizen *See* MOUNTAINEER.

mountain dew An old term for moonshine that has become the name of a nationally known soft drink (when capitalized).

mountaineer See quote. "It provokes them to be called mountaineers, that being a 'furrin word' which they take as a term of reproach. They call themselves mountain people, or citizens; sometimes humorously mountain boomers." (Kephart, *Southern Highlanders*)

mountain grill A derogatory term for a poor white. "[The] world of the mountain grills, the poor whites." (Thomas Wolfe, *The Web and the Rock*, 1938)

mountain hoojy A derogatory term for a HILLBILLY.

mountain ivy Another name for mountain laurel found in hills throughout the mountains. *See* HELL.

mountain people *See* MOUNTAINEER.

mountain shaker A dynamite blast that is heard for miles in every direction.

Mount Bote For an interesting story about how this mountain in the Great Smokies got its name, see the quote following. "In the 1850s a road was built from Cades Cove to the Spence Field on Thunderhead. Since there were no engineers to lay out the route, it was left to the decision of the builders, some of whom were Cherokee, as to which ridge the road should follow. As each Indian was asked his opinion, he reportedly pointed to the westernmost ridge and said 'Bote' to indicate how he voted. There being no V sound in the Cherokee language 'Bote' was as near as they could frame the word; thereafter it was Bote Mountain, while the other ridge, the loser, became Defeat Ridge." (Frome, *High Places*)

Mount Kephart A mountain in the Great Smokies named in his lifetime, a rare honor, for the enigmatic Horace Kephart, who came to live in the Great Smokies and wrote about them and the people that lived in them. Kephart also wrote extensively about camping. In his day he was called the "Grand Old Man of the Campfire and Long Trail."

mourning cloth   Black calico, the cloth traditionally used to line coffins. "The family prepared a fresh coffin of poplar, lined it with mourning cloth."

mouse bush   A charming name hillfolk have for the pussywillow (*Salix discolor*), whose catkins resemble tiny gray mice to some.

mouse in the meal   A variation on the common saying *a fly in the ointment*.

mout   Might. "Say stranger, what mout your name be?" (A. M. Haswell, *A Daughter of the Ozarks*, 1920)

much   To flatter, compliment, praise. "If you don't stop muchin' her all day and night you'll turn her head."

mucher   Farther. "Move it over-there a little mucher."

much of a man   A strong, large or stout man. "You know old Bull is a much of a man." (Stuart, *Beyond Dark Hills*)

mulligrubs   1) Ill temper, surliness, colic. "I knowed in reason she'd have the mullygrubs over the doin's." (Kephart, *Southern Highlanders*) 2) The blues, sadness.

muscle   Often used as a verb, as in "I'll muscle it up (lift it) for you."

music   Can mean a musical instrument, as in, "Bring your music with you when you come," referring to a guitar, etc.

musicker   An old term in the Ozarks for a musician. Also heard as *musicaner*.

my man   A synonym for husband. "My man is the salt of the earth." *See* MY WOMAN.

my woman   A synonym for wife. "My woman will cook supper for us." *See* MY MAN.

nahrr' A pronunciation of *narrow*. "That's a nahrr' road to travel on."

name To call, mention, tell. "They've allers named that thar place the Devil's Garden."

nanny tea An old folk remedy for many ills that isn't used much anymore, if at all. It is made by steeping sheep manure in hot water.

nap o' sleep A redundancy for a nap.

narvish A common pronunciation of *nervous* in the southern Appalachians. *See* quote under DRAP OFF.

nary None, never, neither, not any. "Nary a person came to her party." *See* ARY.

nary'n None, not a one. "'How many people did you kill?' 'I ain't killed nary'n.'" (McCarthy, *Child of God*)

nary-nary Nothing to nothing, as in this Ozark answer giving the score of baseball game: "Nary-nary in the seventh, with we-uns to bat."

nasty To dirty. "Don't nasty my good towels with that mud."

nation A great amount. "She grew a nation of flowers."

natural A severely retarded child. "Their first baby was said to be a natural."

near about Just about, almost, nearly. "He's near about the best runner in this county."

near't Nearly. "She purty near't set the house on fire."

neckid A pronunciation of *naked* in the Ozarks.

needle To have sexual intercourse with. "[She said] I was the nicest boy ever needled her. Needled, for God's sake." (McCarthy, *Orchard Keeper*)

needments Necessities. "We have all the needments of life right here."

negatives See quote.

A double negative is so common [in mountain speech] that it may be crowded into a single word: "I did it the unthoughtless of anything I ever done in my life" . . . [As for] the triple negative: "I ain't got nary none." A mountaineer can also accomplish the quadruple: "That boy ain't never done nothin' nohow." Even the quintuple: "I ain't never seen no men-folks of no kind do no washin." (Kephart, *Southern Highlanders*)

neighbor with   Associate with, bother with. "They don't neighbor with Baptists."

nestes   Nests. The highlander generally drops the *t* in the singular of such words as *nest* and *post*, but pronounces the *t* clearly in the plurals of these words, adding an unaccented syllable so that we have *nestes* and *postes. See* BEASTIES.

nigh   Nearly, near. "He's nigh one-hundred and still works every day."

nighcut   A short-cut. "If we take the nigh cuts, it's about seven miles." (Jesse Stuart, "How Ox Fit," 1940)

nobody's never spied him nohow   Nobody's ever seen him anyway.

nohow   1) In no way or manner. 2) Anyhow. "What air you doin' here nohow?" (Stuart, *Beyond Dark Hills*)

noodle   Apparently deriving from an old Scottish word, to *noodle* means to catch fish with your hands.

norate   To spread news; possibly derives from "narrate." "Go over and norate the district that Pap is dead." (Stuart, "Bury Your Dead")

norated around   Told, gossiped. "It was norated around that he was in prison for life."

North Caroliny   A pronunciation of *North Carolina.* "My great-grandfather on my mother's side . . . settled in the mountains of North Caroliny." (L. N. Roberts, *Cutshin and Greasy*)

not enough room to cuss a cat without gettin' hair in your mouth   Very crowded, like sardines in a can.

nuther   *Neither*, in the Ozarks. "I don't like nuther one."

oak winter Oak leaves are generally late to appear in spring; an *oak winter* is a frost that comes late in spring, after the oaks have small leaves.

odd come short An odd moment, an indefinite period. "One of these odd come shorts I'll do it."

oddling An eccentric. "He's one of God's oddlings."

off-bear Offspring, one's children. "They say he's got more off-bear than anyone in the county."

offcasts Discards. "His kids wear everybody's old offcasts."

offen one's box Crazy, silly, very much mistaken, out of one's mind. "He must have been offen his box to do something like that."

okra Sometimes used by Ozark hillfolk to mean *penis* because of its shape resemblance.

Old Blackie A nickname for the devil. "Watch out or Old Blackie will get you."

Old Boy Another nickname for the devil.

Old Christmas An old-fashioned name for January 6, Twelfth Night or Epiphany, which old-timers celebrated as Christmas.

Old Coaly Still another nickname for Satan. *See* OLD BLACKIE.

olden times Sometimes defined as any time more than two generations back, but usually used in a general way.

Old Gentleman, The Another reverent name for God used by hillfolk.

Old Gyarbro A name for the devil in days past; the origin of the strange name is unknown.

Old Jimson Another nickname for Satan. Possibly suggested by jimsonweed, a poisonous plant.

old-maid gal A redundancy for "old maid." "She's Battle Blevin's old-maid gal Dorey." (Stuart, "Gather-all")

93

Old Master Another reverent name for God used by hillfolk. "Old Master is watching over us."

Old Ned Yet another nickname for the devil.

old none Nothing. "He's got some money but I've got old none."

Old Red A nickname for Satan.

Old Sam Still another of the many nicknames for the devil. Also *Old Sampson.*

Old Scratch Probably the most common nickname for the devil; used in New England and other areas as well.

old-timey Old-fashioned. "She still wears those old-timey clothes."

old Virginia A term sometimes used by older West Virginia speakers for the state of Virginia. "'I was born in . . . old Virginia. And my father brought us to this state [West Virginia].'" (R. E. Thomas, *Come Go With Me*)

on a credit On credit. "He buys everything on a credit." Also *on the credit.*

oncet Once. Mountain people often add a *t* to many words, as in *oncet, twicet, suddent* and *cleft.*

one more time A rousing good time. "We had one more time last night."

onliest Only. "He's the onliest man can do that."

on me On my land. "That fence he put up is right on me."

onset A fight. "It was a master (great) onset between two dogs."

on the cull list Said of a young woman who hasn't married before she is 21 or so, implying that she is undesirable, a cull. "Maryanne is on the cull list."

on the down-go Said in the southern Appalachians of someone or something (a business, etc.) in rapidly declining health. "If declining in health [a man is said to be] on the down-go." (Kephart, *Southern Highlanders*)

on the drop edge of yonder Barely hanging on to life, at the point of death, hanging over the cliff. "There I was, all those tubes and wires fixed to me, hanging on the drop edge of yonder."

ontil A pronunciation of *until.*

oojit-nawsty Apparently deriving from a Cherokee word, this old term means good or pleasing, though it isn't widely used today.

ooze A name for any medicine made of concentrated herbal tea or other substances. "I took some of that ooze she made and felt no better."

opossum has 19 lives See quote. "A saying common among the people of North Carolina, that if a cat has nine lives, the oppossum has nineteen." (*Beadle's Monthly*, July, 1858)

orchard grass A pasture of tall grass or hay.

original Employed by hillfolk to mean any horse with defective sex organs; the term isn't used in mixed company. "I don't want no part of that original."

orphant An orphan, in the Ozarks, a *t* added to the pronunciation, as with *suddent* (sudden), *wisht* (wish) and *cousint* (cousin).

orter A pronunciation of *ought to.* "You orter come to the picnic on Sunday."

Other One, The Another nickname for Satan.

ought to be bored for the simples Said, often fondly, of a stupid person whose mind might be improved by boring a hole in his head to let some of the stupidity drain out. "That fool ought to be bored for the simples."

our contemporary ancestors A designation historians have used to describe the hill people, because the original highlanders came principally from the British Isles and retain many ways of speech common to their and our ancestors.

ourn Ours. "That's ourn land you're on." *See* HOUSEN.

out 1) Off. "The squirrels have been killed out. The timber has been cut." (Stuart, *Beyond Dark Hills*) 2) Often used as a verb meaning to defraud.

outdoingest Most surprising, outrageous. *See* THAT'S THE OUTDOINGEST THING I EVER HURD.

outen Out of. The word may go back to the Anglo-Saxon *utian.* "They know how to drink outen a jug." (Stuart, "Not Without Guns")

outlander A stranger or foreigner to the mountains. "Before you know you'll be fritter-minded as an outlander." (Chapman, *Happy Mountain*) Also *one of the outlandish.*

outlay A quantity purchased or needed. "She wanted an outlay of gingham for a new dress."

out of banks Flooding. See quote. "The river is out of banks." (Stuart, "How Ox Fit")

out of heart Downhearted, discouraged. "He's out of heart since she left him."

outsider See quote. "A bastard is [called] a 'woodscolt' or an 'outsider.'" (Kephart, *Southern Highlanders*)

overbraeden Spread over, overshadow. "The moving light of morning . . . overbraedened the side of Cragg Hill." (Chapman, *Happy Mountain*)

over-fattened on book reading
Used by hillfolk to describe someone
they consider formally over-educated.

overhauls   A pronunciation of *over-alls* still heard in the mountains.

overlay   To kill by suffocation, as in
those tragic cases when an infant's
mother falls deeply asleep in bed atop
her baby and suffocates the child.
"Sick and weary, she fell asleep and
overlayed her precious babe."

overpeer   An overhanging rock.
"An overpeer, from which one would
make a sheer drop." (Chapman,
Happy Mountain)

own cousin   First cousin. "He married his own cousin."

own the corn   Said in the Ozarks
for ACKNOWLEDGE THE CORN.

ozark   Cheat,   defraud.   "He
ozarked her out of her land." The
origin of the term is not known. *See*
OZARKS.

Ozarks   The *Ozark Mountains* in
Missouri, Arkansas and Oklahoma,
ranging up to 2,300 feet high, cover an
area of 50,000 square miles and are
noted more for their beautiful scenery
and mineral springs, which make them
a resort area, than for their rich deposits
of lead and zinc. Also known as the
Ozark Plateau, the *Ozarks* are named
for a local band of Quapaw Indians that
resided in the Missouri and Arkansas
region of the mountains. "The French
were in the habit of shortening the long
Indian names by using only their first
syllables," an article in the St. Louis
Globe-Democrat explains. "There are
frequent references in their records to
hunting or trading expeditions 'aux
Kans,' or 'aux Os,' or 'aux Arch,'
meaning "up into' the territory of the
Kansas, Osage, or Arkansas tribes."
This *aux Arch* seems to be the more
likely explanation for *Ozarks*, although
the local Arkansas band may have been
named from the French *aux Arcs*
meaning "with bows," which could
also have been corrupted to *Ozarks* and
later applied to the mountains where
the Indians lived. Missouri was once
called   the   "Ozark   State."   The
Ozarkian language is the dialect of
Ozark mountain people and includes
many old English and Scottish expressions.

pack To carry. *Carry* is most common in the East and *tote* in the South, but *pack* is the most common term in the Ozarks, as in, "It's too heavy for me to pack around," or "He's packing a pistol."

packing *See* ALL DRUG OUT.

packin' the mail Doing something rapidly, vigorously. "What a race, they were really packin' the mail!"

painter A panther, mountain lion. ". . . they's painters and they's painters. Some of 'em is jest that, and then others is right uncommon. That old she-painter, she never left track once. She wadn't no common kind of painter." (McCarthy, *Orchard Keeper*)

paints her face like a barn Said in the Ozarks of a woman who uses a lot of rouge and lipstick, bringing to mind the color of a red barn.

pair o' beads An old-fashioned Ozark term for a necklace rarely heard anymore. Chaucer used the same term in the *Canterbury Tales*.

pant Sometimes used in the singular to mean *pants*. "He put on his pant backards."

pappy 1) A common name for father, as are *pap, poppy, paw* and *pop*. 2) To father, sire. "Funny how a man so ugly could pappy a gal purty as her." (Stuart, *Trees of Heaven*)

passel A group, many; a pronunciation of *parcel*. "We got a whole passel of them children in Sunday school."

pasture field A pasture. "It was gettin' light enough to see over the pasture fields." (Stuart, "Rich Men")

patch A garden or small piece of land. "That's my tomater patch over there."

paw-pawer A name once commonly given to outlaws or fugitives, from the popular belief that they subsisted in hiding by eating the wild fruit called the paw-paw.

peaked Sick. Pronounced PEAK-ed. "Our little one been pretty peaked recently."

pea-rifle A small-caliber rifle that uses bullets about the size of peas.

peckerwood 1) a woodpecker, usually the red-headed woodpecker. 2) A poor white person.

peeling A spanking. "She gave him a good peeling for disobeying."

peers A pronunciation of *appears*, in the sense of *seems*. "It peers he won't be coming here tomorrow."

pepper duster Heard in the mountains for a pepper shaker.

percoon A pecan or the pecan tree. *See also* PUCCOON.

peter A euphemism for the penis. Vance Randolph wrote in *Dialect Notes* VI, 1928, that "Very few natives of the Ozarks will consider naming a boy Peter" because of this significance. "An evangelist from the North shouted something about the church being founded on the rock of St. Peter," Randolph wrote, "and he was puzzled by the flushed cheeks of the young women and the ill-suppressed amusement of the ungodly. Mountain folk don't even like to pronounce common names like *Hitchcock* or *Cock*."

piece 1) A distance. "We went a short piece." 2) A short period of time. "She's gone quite a piece now." 3) A bit. "I had a little piece of greens

for my dinner, a mess." 4) A contemptuous term for a slovenly careless girl. *See* TABOO WORDS.

pie supper A social fund-raising event where pies and pieces of pie are sold.

pindling Weak and thin or puny. "He's a pindlin' boy."

piney The Ozark name for the flower more widely known as the *peony*. The pronunciation is still a common one. Peonies are also called *piney roses*.

piney roses *See* PINEY.

pink-eye gravy Gravy made from ham and water or milk, named after the red pieces of fat in it. Also called *red-eye gravy*.

pint Point. "Everybody has his good pints."

pizen Poison. "She tried to pizen her man."

pizened A word used for *pregnant* among mountain people. "She got pizened sure enough."

plant the corn before building the fence To get married after a child is conceived. "They planted their corn three months before they built their fences."

playing the red onion Chasing wanton women, *the red onion* meaning the female genitals. "Tommy's been playin' the red onion."

playments Toys and other play-things. *See* PLAY-PRETTIES.

play-party See quote. "A play-party is a square dance without fiddles, or other instrumental music . . . the merrymakers must sing their own songs and make their own mirth." (Wilson, *Backwoods America*)

play-pretties An old term for children's toys. "That girl-child has all the play-pretties you can imagine." *See* PLAYMENTS.

play whaley To make a stupid mistake, blunder badly. "I sure played whaley when I joined the army." An old-fashioned term said to derive from a stupid (perhaps fictional) family named Whaley.

pleasantest day that ever passed over my head The best day I ever experienced; an Elizabethan term that is still heard in the Ozarks.

pleasure To please or indulge in pleasure. "I wouldn't pleasure them enough to say it." (Kephart, *Southern Highlanders*)

pleasures Amuses. "It pleasures me to play with the children."

Plott hound A mountain dog bred for bear hunting, with "bear blood in him." Bred for well over a century by the Plott family of western North Carolina.

plum Very; completely. "He was scared plum to death." Also *plumb*.

plum peach A clingstone peach as opposed to a freestone variety.

plum tuckered out Very tired. "I'm plum tuckered out after all that running." Also *plum beat out*.

pneumonia fever A redundancy for *pneumonia*. "She come down with pneumonia fever last week." Also, *pneumony*.

pod A belly or paunch. "He had some huge pod on him."

pointblank 1) Outright, downright, very. "He looked pointblank awful." 2) A superlative or epithet. "We pointblank got to do it!"

point-blank tale teller An outright liar. "Don't believe anything he tells you—he's a point-blank tale teller."

poke A bag or sack, often one of paper. "We roll our cigarettes in brown sugar poke paper." (Stuart, *Trees of Heaven*) *See also* BAG.

poke supper See quote. "A substitute for the church fair is the 'poke supper,' at which dainty pokes [bags] of cake and other homemade delicacies are auctioned off." (Kephart, *Southern Highlanders*)

pone 1) A loaf of corn bread. "He could eat a whole pone of corn bread." 2) A lump or swelling on the face or body.

'pon my honor! Upon my honor; a common Appalachian exclamation or oath.

poor-hoggin' Living in poverty. "They been poor-hoggin' along the last few years."

poot the rug A term of unknown origin, meaning to die. "They expect he'll poot the rug soon." *See* DON'T AMOUNT TO A POOT.

pop-call A brief visit, on which the visitor just pops in and pops out.

popskull whiskey Cheap, potent moonshine, so named because it seems to pop things inside your skull. ". . . he'd sit with the old man . . . drinking with him from a half gallon jar of popskull whiskey and passing a raw potato back and forth for a chaser . . ." (McCarthy, *Child of God.*)

porched Poached. "She ate two porched eggs for her breakfast."

pore as a rail fence Extremely skinny. "She's pore as a rail fence but very pretty."

pork-meat A redundancy for pork. "We had us some pork-meat and greens."

portly As applied to a man, *portly* means handsome and dignified, not stout or heavy. This meaning goes back to the archaic sense of the word; stately or majestic, a man of substance.

possum grapes A wild mountain grape (*Vitis corifolia*) said to be favored by possums. "In the relative cool of the timber stands, possum grapes and muscadine flourish with a cynical fecundity." (McCarthy, *Orchard Keeper*)

posy-flowers An old-fashioned synonym for a bouquet. "He brought her posy-flowers and candy."

potater A pronunciation of *potato*; also heard as *pertater*.

pour-off A colorful name for a waterfall. "They swam and dove and stood under the pour-off."

pour the rain down To rain very hard. "It's pouring the rain down."

poverty Poverty among hillfolk doesn't mean having little or no money, it means not having *food* or not having enough food, so that one starves to death. "Old James died of poverty out there in the woods."

powerful Very. "That's powerful good whiskey."

powerful ashy Very angry. "Ma's powerful ashy at all of us for not comin' to supper."

powerful cash money A great deal of money. "He had a power of cash money in his money belt."

power of A lot of. "I got a power of things to do."

prank To experiment or manipulate. "Stop prankin' with that choppin' axe."

prayer-bones A humorous term for the knees. "Get down on your prayer-bones and beg his forgiveness."

preaching funeral An old-fashioned term for a funeral held during good weather when the preacher could get to an area; often the person preached over had been dead and buried for nearly a year.

preachment A sermon in church. "The preacher gave a fine preachment."

pretty Can be used as a verb, as in "She prettied herself."

pretty as a new laid egg A compliment for a pretty young woman, someone fresh and bright with beauty.

pretty-by-night A white flower of the southern Appalachians that blooms at night.

prides The male sexual organs. Also called *private parts.*

prince An old-fashioned word that can be used to describe a good, noble woman, just as it was used to describe Queen Elizabeth centuries ago, even after she became queen.

prodjectin' around *See* COOTERIN' AROUND.

professor Heard among hillfolk not for a college teacher, but to describe one who professes his or her faith at a religious revival meeting.

prong Poke, dig, jab. "They laughed and pronged each other in the ribs."

proud 1) Pleased, glad, as in "I'm sure proud to meet you." 2) Said in the Kentucky mountains of a female dog that is excited sexually. *See* BE PROUD.

pruney Filled with sexual desire. *Horny, cagey* and *rollicky* are also so used by hillfolk. "I'm feelin' pruney tonight."

puccoon *See* PERCOON.

puddle jumper An insulting, derogatory name for a highlander. *See* HILLBILLY.

puke An old name for a Missourian. Perhaps a corruption of the earlier name *Pike* for Missouri natives, a name given to them in California because so many Missourians who came there during the gold rush were from Pike County, Missouri.

pukes An attack of vomiting or nausea. "The baby has the pukes."

pumpkin-roller A derogatory term for a country jack, a farmer. "Moonshinin's a man's game. Can't just any pumpkin-roller stick it." (Wilson, *Backwoods America*)

puncheon floor See quote. "'Most of the old houses around Morganton [Arkansas] had floors made out of split [white oak] logs . . . They called that a puncheon floor.'" (R. E. Thomas, *Come Go With Me*)

punish Suffer. "I hate to see him punish like that."

puny Sickly, in poor health. "[She] was feeling right puny-like." (Wilson, *Backwoods America*)

puny feeling Sick. "I been puny feelin' the last week."

pure corn liquor Another name for MOONSHINE.

pure-quill Powerful, undiluted, often said of whiskey. "That's pure-quill moonshine." *See* MOONSHINE.

purty up Beautify, make pretty. "She purtied up for the dance."

pussy Very rustic, awkward. "She's very pussy, comes from back in the woods."

put a fire Make a fire. "He . . . put a fire in the cook stove." (Stuart, *Trees of Heaven*)

put apast Put beyond. "I wouldn't put it apast him to do such a lowdown thing."

put a spider in someone's coffee To poison someone with any kind of poison.

put on a face like a mule eatin' briars To frown painfully. "When she hollered at him, he put on a face like a mule eatin' briars."

put on the cooling board To kill. A *cooling board* is a wide board or plank used in the southern Appalachians and elsewhere to lay out a dead person straight before rigor mortis sets in.

quaggle Used in the central Pennsylvania mountains for "to shake like jelly."

quare Queer, in the sense of odd, strange. "She's a quare old lady who lives far back in the woods."

quarter A fourth of a mile. "He lives up the trail about a quarter." (Wright, *Shepherd*)

quern A mortar for grinding corn once commonly used in the mountains.

quicker'n a snake goin' through a holler log Words describing any rapid movement.

quicklye *See* GOODLYE.

quile To subside, or to quell. "Her pain quiled down by morning."

quill To blow. "He really quilled that whistle."

quit time Quitting time. "About quit time we would watch the sun on the other side of the mountain, and when it got to look like about six inches from the top, we went out." (L. N. Roberts, *Cutshin and Greasy*)

quote Tell, speak. "He quoted him the truth."

quoto A pronunciation of *quota* in the Ozarks.

rabbit's chance Little chance at all. "She had a rabbit's chance of winning the game."

rabbit twister A derogatory name for a backwoodsman; after the way backwoodsmen twist rabbits out of hollow logs with a forked stick. *See* HILLBILLY.

rack To move fast, especially when running. "There he goes rackin' down the road."

Rackensack A humorous derisive name for Arkansas that dates back to the 19th century.

rail-mauling See quote. "'They called it rail-mauling here (in Arkansas). In some other places, they'd call it rail-splitting. It was all the same thing.'" (R. E. Thomas, *Come Go With Me*)

rain crow The yellow-billed cuckoo (*Coccyzus americanus*), whose cry is said to predict that rain is coming. "The rain-crows cry for rain." (Stuart, *Beyond Dark Hills*)

rainin' pitchforks and bull yearlings Phrase describing a very heavy rain.

raised with a tick in his navel Said of someone born and reared in the backwoods.

raise sand To create a disturbance. "He sure raised sand when he got the bill."

raising up Upbringing, childhood. "That was about all the kind of shoes they had back in my grandma's raising up." (L. N. Roberts, *Cutshin and Greasy*)

raisin' Jupiter Raising hell, making trouble. "They were raisin' Jupiter down by the store."

ramp A wild onion or garlic (*Allium tricoccum*) often eaten raw or in salads.

range The usual word for a stove among hillfolk. "She set the pot o' greens on the range to cook."

rat A person who peddles moonshine illegally, on the sly.

raw Naked. "It was so hot they slept raw."

razorback A lean half-wild hog that ranges free in the woods, subsisting on acorns and other foods.

read after Read or read about. "He read after Shakespeare."

reckon Guess, believe, suppose. "I reckon it don't make no differ."

reckon how Wonder. "I reckon how tall he is."

red-combed woman A woman who is sexually excited; the term is said to be based on the bright red comb of a sexually active rooster.

redding Cleaning. "I got me a sight of redding to do tomorrow."

red-eyed Red-handed. "She caught him red-eyed stealin' corn."

red-eye gravy *See* PINK-EYE GRAVY.

red-up To clean the house, put it in order. "I got to red-up before company comes."

redworm An earthworm. "When the redworms came to the top of the ground it was time to go fishing." (Stuart, *Beyond Dark Hills*)

residenter A resident, old resident. "Some of those snakes was old residenters." (Stuart, *Beyond Dark Hills*)

restless as the tip of a cow's tail An old hillfolk saying describing a nerv-ous person. "She's as restless as the tip of a cow's tail."

resty Lazy. "I been feelin' resty all day; must be the heat."

retire A euphemism for "go to bed"; the latter words considered too suggestive of sex among many hillfolk.

revenues Federal government agents who enforce laws against the making of moonshine. "We knowed the revenues and learnt to spot 'em as far as we could see 'em." (L. N. Roberts, *Cutshin and Greasy*)

rhubarb A word for the penis. The expression "The old man couldn't get his rhubarb up" comes from an old folk song.

richere A pronunciation of *right here.* "Come richere."

riddle A centuries-old term for teach or explain still used by hill people. "Riddle me how to do it."

ride and tie Among hillfolk, this is a seldom-used indelicate expression that means the sex act performed by a woman and two men. It is thought to derive from the old practice of two men riding one horse over a great distance: one man rode the horse for a while, tying the horse and walking on until the second man reached the horse, rode it past the second man, etc., until they reached their destination.

ride one bug-huntin' To give one a beating in a fight. "A man that can ride Wash Gibbs a bug huntin' is too blamed good a man t' stay at home all th' time." (Wright, *Shepherd*)

ridge runner A contemptuous term for a highlander. "'Damn ridge runner better back off.' 'I don't call them hillbillies Ridge Runners, I call them Sheep Fuckers.'" (Willis, *Mountains of America*). *See* HILLBILLY.

ridin'-critter An old-fashioned term for a horse or mule. "Man's got to have a ridin'-critter to get around." *See* STABLEHORSE.

rifle-gun A rifle. "My grandmother got the rifle-gun and killed [the bear]." (L. N. Roberts, *Cutshin and Greasy*)

right 1) Long, considerable. "Hit'll take a right spell t' do." 2) All. "Our work is comin' on as right at once." (Stuart, *Trees of Heaven*)

right good Very good. "That's right good pie Aunt Renee McShane made."

right proud to go Very glad to go. "I'd be right proud to go with you to the picnic."

right smart A lot, a considerable amount or distance. "Her place is a right smart piece down the road."

right smart of hardness A great deal of ill-feeling. "There's a right smart of hardness between them."

right uncommon Very unusual. *See* quote under PAINTER.

rile To vex, anger. "He was riled the way Ma talked to him." (Stuart, *Men of the Mountains*)

rimptions Plenty. "We got rimptions of ham meat."

ripshack A Kentucky moutain term for an old saw.

risin' A boil. "I've got a risin' in my year [ear], and hit's about to kill me." (L. N. Roberts, *Cutshin and Greasy*)

river's so low we'll have to start haulin' water to it Used to describe a river in times of drought.

rocenears A pronunciation of *roasting ears*, meaning corn on the cob. "Let's have some of those rocenears tonight."

rode hard and put up wet Overworked, like an overworked horse. "He's rode hard and put up wet."

rollicky *See* PRUNEY.

Rooshians A name given in the Great Smoky Mountains to the wild boar on the theory that they were first imported here from Russia.

rooster A euphemism for a chicken-cock. Other such euphemisms include *crower* and *he-chicken*. *To rooster* means to cock a gun. *See* COCK.

rooster fights An old-fashioned name mountain folk give to violets; the phrase's origin is unknown.

rooster tale Both *cock* and *bull* are TABOO WORDS in the Ozarks, as is the word *tail* (a homophone for *tale*). Thus a rare triple euphemism has arisen in the Ozarks for a cock-and-bull tale. There it is called *a rooster story.*

rose moss Another name for the flower generally known as portulaca.

rotten Often replaces *rot* in mountain talk, as in "They'll rotten afore they ripens."

rotten before he (she) was ripe Sometimes said of a spoiled child. "No wonder he wound up in jail. He was rotten long before he was ripe."

rough'n a cow's tongue Said of someone or something very tough and abrasive.

ruddock Once a common name for the bird known as the cardinal (*Cardinalis cardinalis*), but now rarely used.

ruint Ruined. "He's a ruint man." (Stuart, *Men of the Mountains*)

rullion A coarse man or woman of questionable morals and bad reputation. "He's keepin' that rullion down at the hotel."

run A synonym for a creek, stream or branch, as in *Rocky Run.*

run a sandy To play a trick on someone, to bluff someone. "That's the last time he'll run a sandy on me."

ruther A pronunciation of *rather*. "I'd ruther not go."

ruttin' Mating. "Ruttin' time is over, Buck, for varmints—but by God, not fer you-all."

sack A common term for a cow's udder. *Also see* BAG.

sacked To be jilted by a sweetheart. Pronounced *sackted*. "She sacked him 'cause he drank too much."

safe A cupboard for food storage. "All the dishes fell out of the safe." (Stuart, *Men of the Mountains*)

salat A pronunciation of *salad* familiar to Shakespeare and still used by hillfolk. Words like *ballad, killed, scared* and *held* are pronounced *ballat, kilt, skeert* and *helt*, a *t* replacing the final *d* in them.

salt duster A salt shaker.

salt shake The preferred term for *salt shaker*. "Pass me that there salt shake so I can use it on my corn."

sampler Sample. "He grinned and explained that the [liquor bottle] was a sampler from the latest run." (Wilson, *Backwoods America*)

sandrock Commonly used in the southern mountains for *sandstone*.

sang 1) Ginseng, which is found in the mountains and used to be sold in large quantities to China, where it was first extensively used as a medicine. Also called *sang root*. "He brings in sang [to trade]. Ginseng roots." (McCarthy, *Orchard Keeper*) 2) To hunt for ginseng. "I was just nine years old, and that was the first time I recollect going out sanging. . . . I've been a-sanging ever since. I guess I've dug and sold $10,000 worth, if not more." (L. N. Roberts, Cutshin and Greasy)

sanger 1) A singer. "He was a bass sanger. 2) A gatherer of the ginseng root, often called *sang*.

sangin' Public singing done by local groups of singers. "There's a sangin' tonight at the school house."

sankfield A folk etymology for the flower better known as cinquefoil. "The cattle guards are gone now and the sankfield and dewberry briar have covered up the crossties." (Stuart, *Men of the Mountains*)

sanko To walk quietly and aimlessly. "He sankoed around in the woods all day."

santerin' about *See* COOTERIN' AROUND.

santy pay An Ozark pronunciation of *centipede.*

sartin Certain, especially as pronounced in the Ozarks.

sasser A pronunciation of saucer. "The cat had a sasser of milk."

sassy A pronunciation of *saucy* heard in the Ozarks.

satchel *See* TWITCHET.

saw gourds To snore loudly and consistently while sleeping. "I was exhausted and sawed gourds all night."

saw off a whopper To spin a tall tale, tell a lie.

scadoodles A very large number of. "There's scadoodles of fish in that river."

scarce as preachers in paradise A cynical saying used by some hillfolk. "Deer are scarce as preachers in paradise this year."

scarce-hipped Very thin. "She's just a scarce-hipped little girl."

scarce of Short of, lacking. "They are scarce of money." (Stuart, *Beyond Dark Hills*)

scholar An old term still used in the Ozarks for any student, even a schoolchild.

scoop town! Words said to be a corruption of a Cherokee term that means roughly *Sure!* or *You're damn right!*

scorpion A name given in the hills of North Carolina and Tennessee to the harmless little lizard scientifically known as *Eumeces quinquelineatus.*

scriber An old-fashioned word for a writer, a scribe who writes letters for people, etc. Also *scribe.*

scuttle hole A common term for a hay chute.

sebem A pronunciation of *seven.* "He would be gone from sebem to nine days." (L. N. Roberts, *Cutshin and Greasy*)

second-handed Secondhand. "He bought it second-handed."

seeded The past tense of *see.* "I seeded it happen yesterday."

sellin' pumpkins Making illegal whiskey; an old term dating back to days when bottles of illegal whiskey were hidden in pumpkins sold at the side of the road.

sequoia The largest and tallest living things on earth, the giant sequoias of California and Oregon are named for the exalted Indian leader Sequoyah, a mountain Cherokee who lived in the southern Appalachians. Sequoyah invented the Cherokee syllabary, which not only made a whole people literate practically overnight but formed the basis for many written Indian languages. Sequoyah (also Sequoya, or

Sikwayi) was born about 1770, the son of a white trader named Nathaniel Gist and an Indian woman related to the great King Oconostota. Though he used the name George Guess, he had few contacts with whites, working as a silversmith and trader in Georgia's Cherokee country until a hunting accident left him lame. With more time on his hands, Sequoyah turned his attention to the "talking leaves," or written pages, of the white man and set out to discover this secret for his own people. Over a period of 12 years, ridiculed by family and friends, he listened to the speech of those around him, finally completing a table of characters representing all 86 sounds in the Cherokee spoken language. His system, which he devised by taking letters of the alphabet from an English spelling book and making them into a series of symbols, was adopted by the Cherokee council in 1821, one story claiming that Sequoyah's little daughter won over the council chiefs by reading aloud a message that they had secretly instructed her father to write down. Thousands of Indians would learn to read and write thanks to Sequoyah's "catching a wild animal and taming it," in his own words. The redwood tree (*Sequoia sempervirens*) was named for him not long after his death in 1847. *Also see* CHEROKEE; TRAIL OF TEARS.

serenade A wedding celebration. Also called an *infare*, a *shivaree*.

set To plant a crop of any kind. "He set his corn early this year."

set a bed-spell To stay until bedtime. "Come over and set a bed-spell."

set in to rain Began to rain. "It set in to rain early this morning."

set one's budget down To firmly make up one's mind. "Once I set my budget down I don't waver."

set the fur To humiliate someone. "She sure set the fur on Tom."

set up to Courted. "He set up to her regular."

several In the Ozarks, *several* means not two or three but a large amount.

sew with a hot needle and burning thread An Ozark expression meaning to move hastily.

shacklety Ramshackle, broken down. "They live in that shacklety house down the road apiece."

shacklin' around *See* COOTERIN' AROUND.

shadow-shy Afraid of shadows, especially at night. "'I don't give shucks for moonlight,' exclaimed Cal Royster. 'Give me a black-dark night, when the fox ain't shadow-shy.'" (Kantor, *Bugle Ann*)

sharper 'n a tack Very sharp, bright, especially in business dealings.

she-cow A word heard in the Blue Ridge Mountains for a cow.

shed of Rid of. "I'm sure glad to be shed of him.**"sheep dumplings** A humorous euphemism for sheep droppings or manure.

shelling the woods Campaigning in a town or county before an election. "He's been shellin' the woods here three weeks now hopin' to win."

shelly beans See quote. "[We would put dry beans in the shell or hull] in sacks, get us some big sticks, and . . . bust them hulls up . . . and sort the beans out of the hulls. We called them shelly beans." (L. N. Roberts, *Cutshin and Greasy*)

she's ready to go *See* COCKED.

shet The way hill people pronounce *shut*. "Shet the door before the dog gets out."

shift of clothes A change of clothes. "He ain't got but one shift of clothes."

shiner A moonshiner, one who makes MOONSHINE.

shivaree A ceremony after a wedding. Also called an *infare*, a *serenade*.

shoemouth deep A depth up to the top of one's shoe. "The snow was shoemouth deep."

shootin' fixin's An old Ozark term for guns and pistols. "They had their shootin' fixin's all ready for the Clantons."

shore 1) Sheared. "We shore the sheep today." 2) A pronunciation of *sure*. 3) Shared. "We shore all the money those days."

shortsweetening Sugar. "I like shortsweetening in my coffee."

should ought to A redundancy for *should*. "He should ought to be bored for th' simples." *See* BORED FOR THE SIMPLES.

show 1) Chance. "There ain't much show to get a man." (Wright, *Shepherd*) 2) Often used for *movies*. "We went to the picture show."

showerstick Heard in Arkansas for an umbrella. "Open up that shower stick—it's startin' to rain."

shuckle Hurry, hasten. "They shuckled out of here soon as they seen the sheriff comin'.'"

shummick To lounge about, skip to and fro uneasily. "He stood there shummicking from one foot to the other."

shun out An old term meaning to avoid military service. "'The old home guards would come home, hunting for men that shunned out and were lying out [hiding].'" (R. E. Thomas, *Come Go With Me*)

sich A pronunciation of *such*.

siddlin' *See* ANTIGODLIN.

sight of   A lot of. "We would dry a sight of beans by stringing them and threading them up on strings to dry." (L. N. Roberts, *Cutshin and Greasy*) Also heard as *a sight in the world of*: "The storekeeper dropped the dime in the till and shut the drawer. He said: 'It's a sight in the world of snow, ain't it?'" (McCarthy, *Child of God*)

sight of satisfaction   A satisfying feeling. "Well, hit's a sight of satisfaction to see justice fall." (Furman, *Glass Window*)

signs   Planting signs (the best time to plant a crop), which could be anything from a phase of the moon to aches in various parts of the body. "My father used all the signs in his planting. He planted corn and beans when the sign's in the arms; taters when the sign was in his feet; sowed his cabbage and things like that growed heads when the sign was in the head; planted all his vines when the sign was in the secrets . . . Thy's three days of the year, called barren days, when he wouldn't plant anything." (L. N. Roberts, *Cutshin and Greasy*)

since ever   Often used instead of *ever since*. "Since ever we went there we liked it."

since Heck (Hector) was a pup   A long time ago. "I ain't seen that happen since Heck was a pup."

since the hogs ate my brother up   Heard in the highlands as a humorous way of saying a long time. "Haven't seen you since the hogs ate my brother up."

sink-taller   A whiskey of high proof; so named after the belief that a piece of tallow will sink in liquor of high alcohol content.

skeerce   A pronunciation of *scarce* in the Ozarks. "Meat was skeerce in the winter months."

skeert   *See* SALAT.

skeery-crow   Scarecrow. "Strip off all their fine terbackoo clothes for to make skeery-crows out'n for the pea patch!" (Jesse Stuart, *Basket Dinner*, 1939)

skelped   A common pronunciation of *scalped*.

skillet-an'-led   A Dutch oven, *led* here being a pronunciation of *lid*.

skin a flea for its hide   Exceedingly cheap. "He's been known to skin a flea for its hide."

skin your eyes   Keep a sharp lookout, keep your eyes peeled.

skive   To scrape. "Willard scooted and skived up the grass, cussed, hollered and prayed." (Stuart, "Hangin' of W.B.")

slat   A stick of chewing gum, a term used mainly in the southern Appalachians. "He offered me a slat of his Juicy Fruit."

slathers Lots of, a large quantity. "He's got slathers of money hid all over."

slattery Very dirty, falling apart. "They live in a slattery old house down the road."

sleight Skill, skilled. "Sally's sleight at basketmaking."

slick *See* HELL.

slick as a peeled onion Very smooth and slick, often implying dishonesty. "His scheme was slick as a peeled onion."

slicker To beat or spank severely. "He slickered young Tom something awful."

slink An Ozarkian word meaning to abort a child.

slow as Christmas Slow in coming about.

slowern' sorghum Slower than thick molasses pours, which is quite slowly. "You're slowern' sorgum, Jake."

slut A light made from a saucer of grease with a rag as a wick; origin unknown.

smack out of Have none in supply. "We're smack out of tobacco."

smart To hurt. "Hit haint't a-goin' to smart ye more 'n a minute."

smidgen A very small piece; often used in other regions as well. "He give me a measly old smidgen of the pie."

smothering spell A sudden but not longlasting spell of weakness along with difficult breathing and rapid heartbeat.

snaps A common synonym for string beans in the mountains.

Snawfus This imaginary creature is said to resemble a winged white deer with flowering branches for antlers.

snibbling Weather that is cloudy and rainy. "It's a miserable snibblin' day."

snub To cry or sob. "She's been snubbin' ever since he left her."

sob To soak or sop. "That field is sobbing wet."

sobby Water-soaked firewood; possibly a mispronunciation of *soggy*.

so cold the wolves ate sheep just for the wool An old Ozark saying.

so contrary he floats upstream Said of a very headstrong, stubborn person.

sody A pronunciation of *soda* in the Ozarks. "We had some sody pop to drink."

sog A name for a piece of firewood that doesn't burn properly, just smoldering and turning to charcoal.

some several A lot of. "There's some several deer this season."

soon Early. "They got a soon start before sunrise."

sooner The name for a child born less than nine months after his or her parents were married.

soon start An early start. "Let's get a soon start before everybody else."

sop 1) Gravy. 2) Bread dipped in gravy.

sorghum Commonly used to mean molasses in the Ozarks.

sorgum lapper An insulting, derogatory name for a backwoodsman. *See* HILLBILLY.

sorriest critter on the crick (creek) The poorest specimen of manhood or womanhood around. "He's the sorriest critter on the crick." (Movie version of Wright's *The Shepherd of the Hills*)

sorrow Sorry. "She was sorrow she didn't marry him."

sorry girl A colorful old term for a prostitute heard in Virginia's Blue Ridge Mountains.

sorty Kind of. "The hickery leaves were sorty turning." (Stuart, *Men of the Mountains*)

so stingy he's afeared to set down If he sat down, this saying implies, he'd add wear to the seat of his pants.

sour grape An unusual term for an enemy heard in the Tennessee mountains. "He's been my sour grape for years."

souse Head cheese. "Oh, that souse . . . You took the head of a hog, and feet and ears—and cleaned 'um. And after ye got 'um ready, you cooked 'um till they was perfectly soft. Then you picked all the meat from the bones. Then you either mashed 'um or run 'um through . . . a colander . . . An that was souse. It was just like cheese." (R. E. Thomas, *Come Go With Me*)

sow A word used by hill people to mean a slatternly housekeeper.

spark To court. "I used to go there and spark little blue-eyed Winnie." (Stuart, "Whose Land Is This?")

sparrow-bird A redundancy for sparrow. "He hopped like a sparrow-bird." (Stuart, "People Choose")

sparrowgrass A corruption of *asparagus*, still used by a few old-timers.

speak howdy To greet. "We spoke howdy and traded small talk." (Wilson, *Backwoods America*)

speaking See quote. "Men will travel miles to a speaking (in the southern Appalachians)—which may be a political gathering or one for discussing road building." (J. Thomas, *Blue Ridge Country*)

spear-side The males or menfolk of the family. *See* SPINDLE-SIDE.

spew Strew, cover. "The ground, to use a mountaineer's expression, was all spewed up with frost." (Kephart, *Southern Highlanders*)

spike-nail A thick, long nail. "Willie was so mad at me he could bite a spike-nail in two." (Jesse Stuart, "Betwixt Life and Death," 1939)

spindle-side The females of the family. *See* SPEAR-SIDE.

spittin' snake A reprehensible character. "[He's] the spittin' snake who never came back to see his own wood's colt [illegitimate child]." (Movie version of Wright's *The Shepherd of the Hills*)

splo Another name for MOONSHINE

spouse Applied to a small child among hillfolk, not to a husband or wife. "That little spouse is out working in the field."

sprangle Spread out in twisting lines. "The little branches sprangle out from the creek."

spudding round Ambling about. "She was just spudding round by herself." *See* COOTERN' AROUND.

spunk-water A term for rainwater collected in the hollow stumps of trees.

squack An old name for the gray squirrel. "I'm a-gonna have me some squack stew for dinner."

squack head A fool, a stupid person. *See* CYMBLING HEAD; SQUACK.

squall like a painter (panther) To scream like a panther, very loud.

squander an opinion To gossip idly with someone. "He squandered an opinion with them the better part of a morning."

squire A title once commonly used for a justice of the peace.

squirm like a worm in hot ashes To be very nervous. "When they questioned him about stealin', he squirmed like a worm in hot ashes."

squirmy A colorful term used in the Ozarks for a sprightly young girl.

squirrel-turner An insulting, derogatory name for a mountaineer. *See* HILLBILLY.

squirrel whiskey Another name for MOONSHINE.

stable horse A euphemism for a stallion, which is also called a *ridin' critter*.

stack cakes Pancakes. "I like stack cakes and fried pie and possum."

stallion A taboo word in the Ozarks, where it is often called a STABLE HORSE.

stand A beehive. "Look at the stands of bees my pappie's got." (Stuart, *Men of the Mountains*)

star flower Another name for the common aster flower.

starn A pronunciation of *stern*. "A bumble-bee can't suck the tassels without his starn-end rubbing the ground." (Stuart, *Men of the Mountains*)

starve out Die. This expression, dating back to Elizabethan times, is still used in the Ozarks.

stash Interestingly, the first use of the verb *stash* for hiding something is a 1929 remark about Ozark moonshine: "Billy, he done stashed the jug in the bush an' now the danged old fool can't find it."

stew In the Ozarks, a drink, not a meat and vegetable dish. It consists of hot water, ginger and corn liquor.

stickers *See* FLICKER.

stilling The distilling or making of MOONSHINE.

stink To smell either good or bad. "That stew stinks wonderful."

stir up hell with a long spoon To cause a lot of dangerous trouble. "Fool with his wife and you're stirrin' up hell with a long spoon."

stit Still. "They's stit lots of smoke and dust and I couldn't see too good but I got on up a little ways and directly I seen he's holdin' up somethin'." (McCarthy, *Orchard Keeper*)

stob 1) Stake. "Well, Pa drove a good long stob in the ground whurr he thought they'd be some red worms." (R. E. Thomas, *Come Go With Me*) 2) The jagged stump of a dead tree.

stocking *See* TABOO WORDS.

stodge up To flavor or season with spices. "You got to stodge up that stew some."

stone Many mountain women never use the word *stone* in any sense because one of its old meanings, dating back to early English, is testicle.

stout Strong. "He's stout enough to move it himself."

straddle Heard in the North Carolina mountains for the crotch. "He's wet up to the straddle."

strange Overly nice. "She was acting strange to me and I know she wanted something."

strawberry friend Someone who visits from the city when strawberries are in season, to get free berries from their hillfolk "friends" or relatives.

stretching the blanket Telling a tall tale, exaggerating, lying. "He's known for stretching the blanket a bit."

strut To swell, distend. "His foot was all strutted."

stud 1) Tobacco used to roll your own cigarettes. "He poured out the stud from his sack." 2) Sometimes used for the male of a game fish such as the bass.

studied Thought, figured. "I studied it would be better for me to leave there then . . ." (L. N. Roberts, *Cutshin and Greasy*)

stump To stub, as in "I stumped my toe on the chair."

stumped her toe Said of any married woman who accidentally becomes pregnant. "Little Joe was a cause of her stumpin' her toe."

stump liquor Another name for MOONSHINE.

suade Persuade. "I suaded him to come home."

suck-egg Mean or base. "Well I'll be a suck-egg mule!"

suck the hind tit Get the worst of something, have the worst position. "The workers here been sucking the hind tit for years now."

sudden-quick A redundancy for *suddenly*. "He jumped out of the bushes sudden-quick."

sugar-bread An old word hillfolk use for *cake*.

suddent *See* ONCET.

sugar-liquor A contemptuous term for bourbon made without corn.

sugar orchard The usual term for a sugar maple tree grove.

sull A verb that probably derives from *sullen*. "The old hound's been whupped and he's crawled under the floor and sulled up till he won't come even when you whistle to him to come out."

sullen To act sullen, be sullen. "But when she's a-spittin' like a wildcat or a-sullenin' like a hoot-owl in the cabin, a man ain't got no call to live with her." (O. Henry, "Whiskey of Life," 1903, set in the Cumberland Mountains.)

sun-ball The sun. "I'll be there soon as the sun-ball rises."

Sunday-goin'-to-meetin'-best One's best clothes, those fit to wear to church on Sunday.

sunt A pronunciation of *sent*. "I sunt 'em to the store."

surly Another name for the bull, whose name is considered too coarse and sexual for polite conversation.

surround To make a detour, go around something. "I couldn't git through the laurel; so I jist surrounded it." (Kephart, *Southern Highlanders*)

suspicion Suspect. "I suspicioned him from the start."

swag   1) Sag. "The floor swagged in the center." 2) A depression in the earth.

swallowed a watermelon seed Used by hillfolk to describe a pregnant woman.

swamp dew   Still another name for MOONSHINE.

swan   A form of *swear*, as in "I swan!"

swapped off bad   Badly cheated. "He been swapped off bad."

sweepin' broom   An ordinary household broom used to sweep floors.

sweet   *See* GETTING SWEET.

sweet bubby   The strawberry shrub, *Calycanthus florindus*. So called because of its blossoms' supposed resemblance to female breasts. "Another shrub that belongs to us and eastern Asia and that tempts one to nibble is what the people here call Sweet bubbies. It appears in old-fashioned Northern gardens under the name of sweet-scented or flowering or strawberry shrub." (M. W. Morley, *The Carolina Mountains*, 1913) *See* BUBBY BUSH.

swiddle   Stir, rinse. "She swiddled out her wash."

swinge   Singe. "He had a sensory instinct for rapid and swingeing repartee . . . specimens of the master's [Shakespeare's] swingeing wit." (Wolfe, *Look Homeward, Angel*)

swivet   1) Hurry. "He's in a great swivet to get to the fair." 2) Anxious, fidgety.

swoggle   To stir. "She swoggled her coffee." Also *swiddle*.

swoonded   Swooned. "He swoonded dead away." (J. Thomas, *Blue Ridge Country*)

taboo words Numerous everyday words are avoided by mountain folk whenever possible because they suggest "lustful ideas." Many are treated separately in these pages. Others include, sometimes for no clear reason: *bed, tail, stocking, piece, maiden, bag, buck, bitch, virgin, buckshot, bullfrog, cockeyed, cocksure,* and even *love, heart* and *decent.*

tad A small child, a tot; also *tat.* "Since you was a little *tad.*" (Stuart, *Beyond Dark Hills*)

tahrs A pronunciation of *tires* in the Ozarks.

tail Buttocks, backside. "He'll kick your tail." *See* TABOO WORDS.

take in Begin. "School takes in at nine o'clock."

take in after Chew. "[They] took in after the food with zeal." (Wilson, *Backwoods America*)

take off for the tall timber An old expression meaning to hide oneself from the law in the deep woods.

take sick To fall sick. "I was right over there when he taken sick." (Stuart, *Beyond Dark Hills*)

take the mountain Leave on a journey, hit the trail. "He took the mountain a year ago and we ain't heard from him since."

take to it like a mule to millet To like something very much, like a mule appreciating the taste of millet grass.

take up with anybody's coon dog that will hunt with him (her) To be so lonesome one will be friendly with anyone at all, regardless of how undesirable.

talking Said of a man and a woman considering getting married. "Her mother said they're talking."

talk meeting A social gathering held for conversation. "[They had] Sunday night talk meetings." (Wilson, *Backwoods America*)

talk moonlight To talk nonsense, foolishness. "'You talk moonlight,' Toyster chided his son." (Kantor, *Bugle Ann*)

talk to To court. "He's already talkin' to a girl."

talk to one's plate To say grace at dinner.

tallywags The male genitalia. *Also terriwags.*

tard A pronunciation of *tired* that rhymes with *bard*. "I'm so tard I could sleep standin' up."

tarryhoot Gallivant. "Her husband was tarryhootin' around so much she left him."

tat Tattle, gossip. "I taught you never to tat no tales."

tater A common pronunciation of *potato* in the mountains.

tater-grabber An insulting, derogatory name for a highlander. *See* HILLBILLY.

taw One's dance partner, usually applied to a woman.

teacher-doctor A West Virginia term for a Ph.D., not a medical doctor. "He's a teacher-doctor, not a real doctor."

tear the bone out 1) To leave nothing undone, do something completely. 2) To throw a wild party.

tear the stars out of heaven To go to extremes. "I'll find him if I have to tear the stars out of heaven."

techy "Techy" isn't an ignorant hick pronunciation of *touchy*, as many people believe, for the word (meaning irritable, testy or peevish) is not related to *touch*, but derives from the Middle English *tecche*, a bad habit which in turn comes from the Old French *teche* (a blemish).

teem off Pour off. "Teem off the water from those taters before you mash 'em."

tell it on one's own self Tell a story to others about one's own foolishness. "I remember he used to tell it on his own sef [self] for years and years and laugh jest like anybody." (McCarthy, *Orchard Keeper*)

terbacker *See* BACKER.

termaters Heard in the Ozarks for tomatoes, always in the plural. "A hillman always avoids the singular by some such expressions as 'one o' these termaters'." (Kephart, *Southern Highlanders*)

terriblest Most terrible. "Hit was the terriblest fray ever I seed." (It was the most terrible brawl I ever saw.)

tetchous Very tender and sensitive, touchy. "She's tetchous about everything these days."

thang A pronunciation of *thing*. "'But he'd take that stick, that thang he used, a write. Had a fork in it . . . Yeah, he'd find water.'" (R. E. Thomas, *Come Go With Me*)

thanky Often used to mean *thank you* in the mountains.

thar 1) A common pronunciation of *there*. 2) See quote. "'Where'd you get her from?' the man asked the child. 'Thar was looking for thar,' the child said, and I realized with amazement that she used *thar* for every pronoun . . ." (Patricia Cornwall, *The Body Farm*, 1994, set in the North Carolina mountains)

that-a-way That way. "He went that-a-way up into the trees."

that dog won't hunt Common in the Ozarks and elsewhere for anything, especially a plan or idea, that won't work, that isn't practical. "It looks good on paper, but that dog won't hunt."

that's how the cow ate the cabbage An expression hillfolk use to indicate that the speaker is laying it on the line, telling it like it is, getting down to brass tacks—with the connotation of telling someone what he or she needs to know but probably doesn't want to hear. According to Little Rock attorney Alston Jennings, who submitted this term to Richard Allen's February 2, 1991, "Our Town" column in the *Arkansas Gazette*, the expression has its roots in a story about an elephant that escaped from the zoo and wandered into a woman's cabbage patch. The woman observed the elephant pulling up her cabbages with its trunk and eating them. She called the police to report that there was a cow in her cabbage patch pulling up cabbages with its tail. When the surprised police officer inquired as to what the cow was doing with the cabbages, the woman replied, "You wouldn't believe me if I told you!"

that's the out doingest thing I ever hurd That's the most surprising thing I ever heard.

that's your lookout That's your business, you take care of it.

that there That. "Fetch me that there wood and then fetch some water."

theirselves Themselves. "They caught the coon theirselves."

them The plural pronoun *them* is often employed with several singular nouns that are considered plural, such as "them molasses," "them cheese" and "them lettuce."

there's another verse to that song You've only presented one side of the story.

there's squirrel in the tree somewhere Something's hidden, there's something more to a situation than meets the eye at first glance.

there's somethin' dead up the branch Something's strange, something's rotten in Denmark. A branch is a stream of water.

there's two sides to every flapjack There's two sides to every question.

thesehere A redundancy for here. "All these here fixy contrapshuns." (J. Thomas, Blue Ridge Country)

they Often used for "there" in the Ozarks, as in "They're too many dang fool laws."

they-all They. "They-all live up the road apiece."

they'll fight at the drop of a hat and they'll drop it themselves A colorful expression describing very contentious, violent people.

thick as dog hair An Ozark expression meaning too crowded, like crops that are planted too close together. "That corn is thick as dog hair, got to thin it out."

thicker'n warts on a pickle Hillfolk use this expression to describe anything abundant, as the bumps are on pickles.

thinks he (she) hung the moon Thinks very highly of someone, thinks he or she is a very important person. Used throughout the South as well. "She thinks Gerry hung the moon when it comes to music."

this day and time This era, period of time. "Pleonasms are abundant [here], such as 'In this day and time.'" (Kephart, Southern Highlanders)

this here This. "This here little jug is mine."

this town's so tough the sheriff has to hire a bodyguard A humorous remark heard in the Ozarks.

thoughted A word describing someone thoughtful of the feelings of others. "You'll find he's a thoughted man."

thousands Often used in reference to size instead of as a number. "This dress is thousands big on me."

three hundred and sixty degree son of a bitch See quote. "No, those were sorry people all the way around, ever man jack a three hundred and sixty degree son of a bitch, which my daddy said meant they was a son of a bitch any way you looked at them." (McCarthy, Child of God)

through 1) The number of rows field hands work through a field. "Twenty rows of corn at a through and this cornfield surely fades." (Stuart, Men of the Mountains) 2) A church meeting shouting spell. "This ungovernable shouting, body conversations, etc., is called 'taking a big through'." (Kephart, Southern Highlanders) 3) Heard in the North Carolina mountains for a spasm. "He had a big through of snapping." 4) A series of medicine doses. "He took a through of calormel last week."

tiddy-bit A small portion. "I had a tiddy-bit of ham for dinner."

tide A flood or freshet. "A spring tide will stop all travel, even from neighbor to neighbor." (Horace Kephart, The Mountain Dialect, 1922)

tight as the bark on a hickory log Very cheap. "Jonas is tight as the bark on a hickory log."

time of books A period in school when the students are studying rather than being taught or playing.

toad strangler A very heavy rain. Synonyms are a *goose-drownder* and a *fence lifter*.

toddick A small amount. "Ben didn't git a full turn o' meal, but just a *toddick*. This meal he measures out in a doll-dish or toddick or taddle." (Kephart, *Southern Highlanders*)

to-do Ado. "It's much to-do about nothing."

tolable A pronunciation of *tolerable*, though its meaning is "mediocre."

tole To entice; a word dating back before Shakespeare that highlanders still use. "She tole him on."

tomatoeses *See* BAKING POWDERS.

tomfuller A synonym for hominy that is said to derive from an old Cherokee word.

tonguery An old term heard in the southern mountains for *gossipy*. "She's a tonguery woman."

too big for her clothes A euphemism for a pregnant woman.

took out To leave quickly, abruptly. "He took out for the hills."

toothbrush See quote. "A twig or two of sweet birch, chewed to shreds at one end was her 'toothbrush'—a snuff stick." (Kephart, *Southern Highlanders*)

tooth-dentist A redundancy for "dentist" still heard in the North Carolina mountains.

tooth jumper A humorous, old-fashioned name for a dentist.

tooth-jumping The extraction of a tooth by holding a nail at an angle against it and striking the nail with a hammer so that the tooth jumps out. Once a common practice in the mountains.

top cow A term for a bull in the Ozarks; not used in the presence of women, when *cow brute* is sometimes substituted.

tore-downdest 1) The worst. "That's the tore-downdest house I ever seen. 2) Toughest, most overpowering. "He's the tore-downdest man I ever knew."

tote *Tote*, though it is of uncertain origin, may come from the African Kenya language *tota*, to carry, from which it passed into Gullah dialect and came to be widely used in the South, including the mountain areas.

tote fair To do the right thing, do the ethical thing. "I aim to tote fair with everyone."

tother A pronunciation of *the other*. "I don't want one or tother."

touch hands Come together, help each other, cooperate on a project. "If we all touch hands, we can get this done."

tourister Often describes a tourist or someone on vacation in the mountains.

tow sack Commonly used to mean a burlap bal.

trace A southern Appalachian word for a creek, a branch or fork of a stream.

traffickin' about *See* COOTERIN' AROUND.

Trail of Tears Some Cherokees managed to escape this terrible unlawful eviction by hiding in the mountains, but most were forced to leave their ancestral homes and many died in a death march that became known as the Trail of Tears. "Tears came to his own eyes when he spoke of that blot on southern civilization, The Trail of Tears, in which the Cherokees, a peaceful and home-loving Indian tribe, were torn [1838–39] from the land which a government had given them by sworn treaty to be sent far away on a march which, from cold, hunger, exposure, and heartbreak was marked by bleaching bones from Georgia to Oklahoma." (Edna Ferber, *Cimarron*, 1930) *See* CHEROKEE; SEQUOIA.

tread 1) A step. "Watch that broken tread on the staircase." 2) To copulate; a word taboo when women are present. "He's been treadin' all the widders in town."

tree To drive an animal up a tree, usually with hunting dogs. Such a dog is often called a *tree hound*. "Black-Boy [a dog] would tree." (Stuart, *Beyond Dark Hills*)

triflin' Lazy. "He's slow and triflin'."

trollup A Scotticism heard in the North Carolina mountains for a slovenly woman.

tryin' to cut a big hog with a little knife Undertaking a job without the proper tools.

tuck A pronunciation of *took*. "They tuck their time getting her."

Tuckahoe Any Virginian living east of the Blue Ridge Mountains. "Generations of his people have been Tuckahoes."

tuckered out Tired. "I get tuckered out tryin' to keep up with him."

tunk Thump. "Tunk that melon to see if it's ripe."

turkey-mouthed Hillfolk hunters use this term to describe a hunting dog with an inadequate voice. "Reckon it is a bit turkey-mouthed for one of ours." (Kantor, *Bugle Ann*)

turkeytailed Hurried, ran. "He turkeytailed it for home."

turkle A name sometimes given to the snapping turtle.

turn A load of wood, coal, etc. "I saw Williburn going to town with a turn of corn on his back." (Stuart, *Men of the Mountains*)

turned off colder Became colder. "When he got home it was past midnight and had turned off colder yet." (McCarthy, *Orchard Keeper*)

turn off Turn out. "You certainly can turn off the work." (Stuart, *Beyond Dark Hills*)

turn over the gravel Said of a man in good health, indicated by his ability to urinate so vigorously he can turn over gravel on the ground.

turr An Ozark pronunciation of *terror*, just as *error* is pronounced *urr*.

tutor To spoil or pamper. "She tutored that child till he turned out bad."

twicet *See* ONCET.

twinkles Heard in the North Carolina mountains and elsewhere for pine needles or spruce needles.

twistification An old-fashioned term for a country dance. "Tom wanted to ask Alice to the church twistification."

twitchet The female pudendum, which is also called the *monkey, moosey* and *satchel,* among more common names.

ujinctum Heard in the North Carolina mountains as a synonym for hell.

ummern *See* DUMMERN.

unbeknowns Unbeknown, unknown. "Sabrina comes unbeknowns and she leaves unbeknowns." (Stuart, *Trees of Heaven*)

unbounded Broke. "You unbounded your word to me."

unliving An archaic compound word still used by highlanders for *dead*.

unquile Uncoil. "[The snake] unquiled, it kep unquilin'." (Stuart, "When Foxes Flirt")

unthoughtless Very thoughtless, callous. "I did it the unthoughtless of anything I ever did in my life." (Kephart, *Southern Highlanders*)

up and done it Went and did something. "We told him not to, but Will up and done it."

up-and-gone-person Someone who changes jobs frequently, or moves his residence from here to there.

upheaded 1) Holding one's head high. "She's some fine lookin' upheaded gal." 2) Intelligent. 3) Cunning, shrewd.

uphold for To stand up for someone. " Dark Hills)

up in See quote. "He must up in eighty [in his eighties]," (Stuart, *Trees of Heaven*)

up-in-G An old term sometimes said of high-class people; the term's origin is unknown.

uppity Conceited. "She's the most uppity gal I ever met."

up to the shoe mouth Up to the opening at the top of a shoe. "The snow is up to the shoe mouth." *See* SHOEMOUTH DEEP.

urn A pronunciation of *yearn*. "I urn to see her again."

urrant The usual pronunciation of *errand* in the Ozarks.

use Can be employed to mean *inhabit.* "Day afore to hunt we usually go up to find where the bears are a-using." (Frome, *High Places*)

used to could Used to be able to. "Why I used to could sing some of 'em [folk songs]." (L. N. Roberts, *Cutshin and Greasy*)

usen Heard in the highlands for "used." "I wouldn't buy those old usen clothes."

usings Products or goods one uses for oneself rather than sells. "That's why we had only 65 bushels of potatoes to sell above our usins." (Stuart, *Trees of Heaven*)

Valley A name, always capitalized, for the great Shenandoah Valley between the Blue Ridge and the Allegheny Mountains. "We're headed for the Valley."

vasty An old synonym for "vast" not much heard anymore.

vault To hide something securely. "He vaulted his money under the floorboards."

vigroush Used by Ozark hillfolk to mean vicious or dangerous. "He's a vigroush man you'd best stay away from."

virgin *See* TABOO WORDS.

vittles Food. "I need to et my vittles on time."

volunteer A euphemism for an illegitimate child among hillfolk. Possibly based on garden plants called volunteers that spring up in unexpected places. *See* WOOD'S COLT.

vomick Vomit. The final *t* in this word is often pronounced like a *k*.

W

waddle To form into a wad. "He waddled his cud of tobacco behind his jaw." (Stuart, "People Choose")

wadn't A pronunciation of *wasn't*. "He wadn't there tonight."

waistie An old-fashioned word for a waist or shirt in the Ozarks.

waiter The best man at a wedding, though the term once meant a bridesmaid as well. "John was waiter to his brother at his wedding."

walk in the wind A synonym for "walk on air." "It must be a dream I was dreaming! I walked in the wind for three days." (Stuart, *Beyond Dark Hills*)

wall To roll one's eyes, showing the whites. "Ma walled her eyes back. She was comint to." (Stuart, "Bury Your Dead")

wampus A mythical creature of the mountains. "She told him that the night mountains were walked by wampus cats with great burning eyes and which left no track even in snow, although you could hear them screaming plain enough of summer evenings." (McCarthy, *Orchard Keeper*)

war A pronunciation of *were*. "We war all goin' to the picture show."

warnut Walnut. "Most of the materials were colored brown, having been dyed with walnut hulls (also known as warnuts)." (Frome, *High Places*)

warrant Guarantee. "'I'll warrant you,' his father replied." (Kantor, *Bugle Ann*)

wash-off A bath in a washtub in which the bather stands erect and washes himself with soap and a washcloth.

wassy Heard in the Ozarks for a wasp.

waste A synonym for spend or use, not squander, in the southern Appalachians.

watchin' his bees A euphemism in the southern mountains for a man expecting his wife to have a baby, waiting for the baby to be born. "John's watchin' his bees a week now." Also *waitin' for his bees to swarm.*

wawsh Wash. "I've got to do my weekly wawsh down by the creek."

wax The word for chewing gum in the Ozarks. *Gum* there means a rabbit trap. "Let me have a stick of that wax." *See* GUM.

weaked Wicked. "Pappie lived a wild weaked life." (Stuart, *Trees of Heaven*)

we-all We. "[A corporation] lapsed into southern mountain talk. Thomas J. Watson, president of I.B.M., took full-page advertisements in the papers to proclaim: "I" represents only one person. "We" may mean only two or a few persons. Our slogan now is WE-ALL . . . President Roosevelt, our Commander-in-Chief, can be certain that WE-ALL are back of him." (*Time*, January 12, 1943)

we-alls Sometimes used by hill people for *we,* usually in the possessive case. More generally WE-ALL.

wear out Give a beating to. "'. . . I wished many a time I could jist . . . get me a good switch and wear you out.'" (R. E. Thomas, *Come Go With Me*)

wearying Worrying. "She is always wearying about something."

weather To storm. "Looks like it's goin' to weather soon."

weed-bender An insulting, derogatory name for a mountaineer.

weedmonkey A prostitute; a loose woman. "I messed around with every weedmonkey in this town." (Stuart, *Beyond Dark Hills*)

weight Weigh. "I don't weight but 120 pounds." (Stuart, *Men of the Mountains*)

well broom me out! An old-fashioned exclamation in the Ozarks.

well fixed Wealthy. "He's a well-fixed man."

well, fry me brown! A euphemism for *Well, I'll be damned!*

well, I'm fexatiously whipped out! I'm completely surprised, *fexatiously* here probably is a variation of *vexatiously.*

West-by-God-Virginia A humorous name for West Virginia, said to have been coined by an irate native when it was said he came from Virginia. Replied the man: "Not Virginia, but WEST, by God!, Virginia!"

West Virginia West Virginia is composed of 40 western mountain counties that seceded from Virginia at the outbreak of the Civil War, these counties voting not to secede from the Union and forming their own state government. After rejecting the names New Virginia, Kanawha, and Alleghany, the new state settled on West Virginia, an ironic choice, as Virginia extends 95 miles farther west than West Virginia does. West Virginia had considered seceding from Virginia several times, due to unequal taxation and representation, and the Civil War provided an excellent excuse. Its constitution was amended to abolish slavery and President Lincoln proclaimed West Virginia the 35th state in 1862, justifying his action as a war measure. Called the "Panhandle State," it has an odd outline, leading to the saying that it's "a good state for the shape it's in."

West Virginny West Virginia. "He's from West Virginny." (Marjorie Kinnan Rawlings, *South Moon Under*, 1933)

whack To tell a tall tale or white lie. "He was really whackin' when he told you that one."

whar Where, but often pronounced *whur* as well. *See* WHUR.

what-all What. "What-all was that blamed thing?"

wheelhorse A tireless, dependable worker. "There's more wheelhorses in the world than big wheels."

whenever Sometimes used to mean *when*. "Whenever I was young, I listened to my parents."

when the hoot owl hollers at noon Used to describe a distant place, so deep in the dark woods that the owls can't tell day from night.

where Often employed as a relative *which* or *who*. Though not consistently used in this fashion, *where* is sometimes heard in sentences like "That old water where comes out of a fasset (faucet)."

whichaway Which way. "'We'd see whichaway they [the bees] was a-goin' back to their trees.'" (R. E. Thomas, *Come Go With Me*)

whiffle-bird A bird of Ozark folklore that flies backward, never forward.

whilst An old-fashioned word for *while* still used by hillfolk.

whippoorwill storm Any late spring storm with heavy winds.

whistle pig A common old name for what is elsewhere called a groundhog or woodchuck.

whitefish See quote. "Most hillfolk do not eat mushrooms, but those that do usually call them whitefish—perhaps because they roll them in cornmeal and fry them in deep grease, like fish." (Vance Randolph, "A Word List from the Ozarks," *Dialect Notes*, 1926)

white lightning Another name for MOONSHINE.

white-livered widder Any woman who outlives several husbands and remains in good health herself. No one knows what fact, if any, is behind the superstition of the "white liver."

white mule Another name for MOONSHINE.

who-all Who. "Who-all was at the meeting?"

[does something to] who laid the chunk Does something better than anyone else; the origin of the expression is unknown. "She raises hogs to who laid the chunk."

whoop owl A hoot owl or any loud owl.

whup A common pronunciation of *whip*. "He whupped that old horse to make it move."

whur A pronunciation of *where*. "'And she finally—she burnt it, whur it was a-clawing up right under the cookstove, a-trying to claw a hole big enough to get in the house." (R. E. Thomas, *Come Go With Me*)

whut A common pronunciation of *what*.

widder, widdy A frequent pronunciation of *widow*. "I saw the widder Perkins tother day."

widow and orphan maker A name the mountaineers gave to the famed Pennsylvania rifles, which they used in the Battle of New Orleans.

wild pork Bear meat. "'The way to cook wild pork is: drap several hot rocks in a pot o' bilin' water with the meat for several hours. Then, throw the meat away and eat the rocks." (Frome, *High Places*)

willipus-wallupus A huge imaginary monster of the mountains invoked to frighten strangers or children.

winder lites Windowpanes. "One of the winder lites is broken."

windy A false, humorous story not intended for anyone to take seriously, a tall tale.

wing To court. "He's been wingin' her two years now."

winter fever An old-fashioned term for pneumonia. "He came down with a nasty case of the winter fever."

wishful-like Wistfully. "She sat there wishful-like."

wisht *See* ORPHANT.

withey Tough and wiry. "He's a withey little feller."

with socks on Coffee with milk and sugar added. "I'll take my coffee with socks on." *See* BAREFOOTED.

with squirrel An Ozarkian synonym for pregnant or *with child*; perhaps a woman carrying an active child suggested someone with a squirrel in her belly, but the origin of the term is unknown.

womenfolks The females of a family. *See* SPINDLE-SIDE.

wonderful Hillfolk often use the adjective to describe something terrible, as in "It was a wonderful storm destroyed the school."

won't nothin' make, won't nothin' keep Said of crops during bad weather. "They's a good warm spell comin' on. Won't nothin' make, won't nothin' keep." (McCarthy, *Orchard Keeper*)

won't pass without pushing' Is inferior, substandard. "That won't pass without pushin.'"

woodchuck Woodpecker, because of the *pecker* in its name, is a taboo word in the Ozarks, where a woodpecker is euphemistically called a woodchuck.

woodpecker *See* WOODCHUCK.

wood's colt A kind euphemism for an illegitimate child among mountaineers. *Wood's Colt* is the title of a book published in 1933 by Thames Williamson and written entirely in mountain dialect. *See* BORN ON THE WRONG SIDE OF THE BLANKET; VOLUNTEER.

wool To worry. "That baby wooled that pore little kitten plumb to death."

wooly heads *See* HELL.

wored Wore. "He wored the same clothes every day."

workbrickle A good worker. "One workbrickle is worth three of you."

workingest *See* MOANINGEST-FULLEST.

worser Worse. "He's gotten worser every day."

wouldn't pass without pushin' Said of anything inferior. "That shovel wouldn't pass without pushin'."

wowser This imaginary panther of the mountains kills cattle and other livestock by biting off their heads with a single bite.

wrastle The way Ozark hillfolk pronounce *wrestle*.

wrench A pronunciation of *rinse*. "Let me wrench out those clothes for you."

writ Wrote, written. "The sweetest words ever writ." (Stuart, *Men of the Mountains*)

write when you get work Common parting words to those leaving the mountains to look for employment.

written Wrote. "He written his son a letter."

wrop Wrap. "She wropped that package."

X The capital letter *X* was once widely used in the southern mountains and other parts of the South to mean a 10-dollar bill, as in "I haven't got an X left." *XX*, or *double X*, meant a 20-dollar bill.

xter A common pronunciation of *extra*. "I did some xter work for you today." Sometimes spelled *exter*.

xtry *See* EXTRY.

XX *See* X.

yaller janders Yellow jaundice, as pronounced in the southern Appalachians.

yaller patches *See* HELL.

yander Yonder. "'I live over yander.' She motioned vaguely beyond the creek." (McCarthy, *Orchard Keeper*)

yank Another name for the bird better known as the nuthatch (*Sitta carolinensis*), probably because its blue coat suggested the Yankee uniform of the Civil War.

Yankee bump Heard in the Ozarks for a bump or depression in a road. *See* LOVE HOLE.

yapped up Messy. "The house is all yapped up."

yar *See* HYAR.

yarnin' Complaining. "He's always a-yarnin' about money."

ye Sometimes used for *you*. "'Say now,' he said, 'you don't have any, uh . . . tire pumps, do ye?'" (McCarthy, *Orchard Keeper*)

year A pronunciation of *ear*. "We used a medicine called sweet oil for the yearache." (L. N. Roberts, *Cutshin and Greasy*)

yeaw A pronunciation of *yeah* or *yes*. "Yeaw, he stayed around with us some and I've talked to him a lot." (L. N. Roberts, *Cutshin and Greasy*)

yellow hammer A name for the golden-winged woodpecker (*Colaptes auratus*).

ye'ns You. "He held his hands to the fire and looked casually about. 'Cold enough for ye'ns?' he said." (McCarthy, *The Orchard Keeper*)

yestiddy A common pronunciation of *yesterday*. "It was raining hard, a real gully washer, yestiddy."

Y-God! *See* I-God!

ying-yang According to Welden Stone in his novel *Devil Take a Whittler* (1948), *ying-yang* is a synonym for the penis.

yins A shortening of *you ins* (you ones), which means *you*. "Well, I reckon I better get on. We'll see yins." (McCarthy, *Orchard Keeper*)

yit Yet. "I've not got into that corn up yander yit." (L. N. Roberts, *Cutshin and Greasy*)

yo A female sheep. In the Ozarks the word (a corruption of *ewe*) is pronounced to rhyme with *woe*.

yokum *See* HALF-BAKED YOKUM.

yooper An affirmative interjection meaning "You bet!" or "Yes, sir!", as in "Are we winning? Yooper!"

yopped up Messy. "This house is all yopped up."

you-all The plural of you. *You-all* (often pronounced *y'all*) is widely considered the *ne plus ultra* of Southern dialect and is most common in the southern mountains. But this expression, used throughout the South, is much misunderstood. Mainly applied to two or more people, *you-all* can be used when the speaker is addressing one person, but only when the sentence implies plurality. Except for some speakers in the Ozarks and rural Texas, only a ham of a stage Southerner would use *you-all* so indiscriminately as to say "That's a pretty dress you-all are wearing." But any Southerner might well say "How you-all?"—the question intended to inquire of the health of you and your entire family or group. Further, the inflection of the phrase is all impor-

tant. When the *you* in *you-all* is accented, as in "*You*-all must come," this means that the group near the speaker is invited. The contraction of *you-all*, *y'all*, is always used in this plural sense. Recently the American Southernism *y'all* (or *yawl*) has been explained, though hardly to the satisfaction of everyone, as a "calque" (a filling in of an African structure with English material) from the West African second person plural *unu*, which is also used in the American black Gullah dialect. This theory is advanced in a study by Jay Edwards in Hancock and Decamp's *Pidgins and Creoles* (1972): "In the white plantation English of Louisiana the form *y'all* (semantically *unu*) was probably learned by white children from black mammies and children in familiar domestic situations." In any case, the closest thing that has been found in English to the collective second person plurals *you-all* and *you-uns* is the collective second person *you-together* that is sometimes heard in England's East Anglia dialect today.

you all's Your. "I saw you all's wagon on the road yesterday."

you can't keep a squirrel on the ground It's futile to force someone to do something he's not naturally suited to do.

you come Come again; words often said in parting company with people.

your-all Your. "Those are your-all dogs." (Wilson, *Backwoods America*)

your happy tootin'! An exclamation meaning "You're right." "Your happy tootin'!" (Stuart, "Not Without Guns")

yourn Yours. "Well, he's yourn then. You can take him home with ye . . ." (McCarthy, *Orchard Keeper*). *See* HOUSEN.

your un's Your. "Let's we-uns all go over to your un's house." (Kephart, *Southern Highlanders*)

you-uns You, singular and plural. "You-uns come down with me." (Kephart, *Southern Highlanders*) The much-ridiculed *you-uns* of mountain speech can actually be traced to the *ye ones* of Chaucer's time, and the collective second person *you-together* is sometimes still heard in British East Anglia dialect. *See* YOU-ALL.

youth "The new moon ull youth to-day"—that is, a new moon will appear or be born.

yowe Ewe. "He was tall like a bean-pole, with a yowe neck." (Stuart, *Men of the Mountains*) Also *yo*.

yown Yours. "It's yown, not mine."

zany Commonly used as a synonym for a clown in the Ozarks.

zat Is that. "Who zat up on the hill?"

zip An old term for molasses. "I'd like some zip on my vittles." *See* 'LASSES.

zoon To fly or run fast with a humming or buzzing sound. The term seems to be confined to the South. "They zooned up into the hills."

About the Author _____

ROBERT HENDRICKSON is the author of more than 25 books, including several critically acclaimed works on language and literature. For Facts On File he has written *American Literary Anecdotes, British Literary Anecdotes* and *World Literary Anecdotes,* as well as *Whistlin' Dixie, Happy Trails* and *Yankee Talk.* He is also the author of *The Facts On File Encyclopedia of Word and Phrase Origins, Revised and Expanded Edition.* He lives in Peconic, New York.

Other volumes in the Facts On File Dictionary of American Regional Expressions series are *Whistlin' Dixie: A Dictionary of Southern Expressions* (0-8160-2110-4), *Happy Trails: A Dictionary of Western Expressions* (0-8160-2112-0) and *Yankee Talk: A Dictionary of New England Expressions* (0-8160-2111-2 [hc]; 0-8160-3507-5 [pbk]). Forthcoming is a volume on New York expressions (0-8160-2114-7).